Every failure of Truth to persuade
reflects the weakness of its advocates.

ARISTOTLE

If you continue in my word,
you are truly my disciples;
and you will know the truth,
and the truth will make you free.

JESUS

WHY GOOD
ARGUMENTS
OFTEN FAIL

MAKING A MORE PERSUASIVE CASE FOR CHRIST

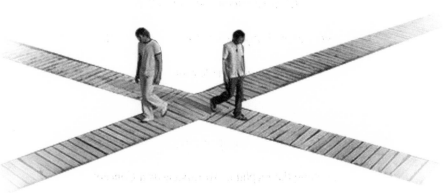

JAMES W. SIRE

IVP Books

An imprint of InterVarsity Press
Downers Grove, Illinois

Inter-Varsity Press

Leicester, England

InterVarsity Press, USA
P.O. Box 1400, Downers Grove, IL 60515-1426, USA
World Wide Web: www.ivpress.com
Email: mail@ivpress.com

Inter-Varsity Press, England
38 De Montfort Street, Leicester LE1 7GP, England
Website: www.ivpbooks.com
Email: ivp@ivp-editorial.co.uk

©2006 by James W. Sire

InterVarsity Press®, USA, is the book-publishing division of InterVarsity Christian Fellowship/USA®, a student movement active on campus at hundreds of universities, colleges and schools of nursing in the United States of America, and a member movement of the International Fellowship of Evangelical Students. For information about local and regional activities, write Public Relations Dept., InterVarsity Christian Fellowship/USA, 6400 Schroeder Rd., P.O. Box 7895, Madison, WI 53707-7895, or visit the IVCF website at <www.intervarsity.org>.

Inter-Varsity Press, England, is the publishing division of the Universities and Colleges Christian Fellowship (formerly the Inter-Varsity Fellowship), a student movement linking Christian Unions in universities and colleges throughout Great Britain, and a member movement of the International Fellowship of Evangelical Students. For information about local and national activities write to UCCF, 38 De Montfort Street, Leicester LE1 7GP, email us at email@uccf.org.uk, or visit the UCCF website at www.uccf.org.uk.

Chapter one, "Love Is a Fallacy," is reprinted from The Many Loves of Dobie Gillis, © 1951, 1979, by Max Shulman with the permission of the Harold Matson Co., Inc.

Scripture quotations, unless otherwise noted, are from the New Revised Standard Version of the Bible, copyright 1989 by the Division of Christian Education of the National Council of the Churches of Christ in the USA. Used by permission. All rights reserved.

Design: Cindy Kiple
Images: Windsor & Wiehahn/Getty Images

USA ISBN-10: 0-8308-3381-1
    ISBN-13: 978-0-8308-3381-8
UK ISBN-10: 1-84474-136-2
    ISBN-13: 978-1-84474-136-6

Printed in the United States of America ∞

Library of Congress Cataloging-in-Publication Data

Sire, James W.
    Why good arguments often fail: making a more persuasive case for
Christ/James W. Sire.
      p. cm.
    Includes bibliographical references and index.
    ISBN-13: 978-0-8308-3381-8 (pbk.: alk. paper)
    ISBN-10: 0-8308-3381-1 (pbk.: alk. paper)
    1. Jesus Christ—Person and offices. 2. Apologetics. I. Title.
BT203.S5 2006
239—dc22
                                                                    2005033146

British Library Cataloguing in Publication Data

A catalogue record for this book is available from the British Library.

P	18	17	16	15	14	13	12	11	10	9	8	7	6	5	4	3	2	1
Y	21	20	19	18	17	16	15	14	13	12	11	10	09	08	07	06			

To my friends at Starbucks

where my arguments fail much too often

CONTENTS

ACKNOWLEDGMENTS

It would be impossible for me to acknowledge all the people who have contributed to the current form of this book. It is based on a lifetime of contact with people from all walks of life and from many different countries. I think of all the students and others who have attended my lectures throughout the universities of North America and much of Eastern Europe. Dialogue with them has been rich in personal impact and molded my mind well beyond my imagination. The greatest contribution, though, has been made by those with whom I have taught in colleges and seminaries and worked alongside as editor. Countless conversations with faculty colleagues and students, campus staff members with InterVarsity Christian Fellowship, authors and fellow editors, intellectual friends and Starbucks buddies: all of these have contributed in ways I have no way of knowing.

Still, I can list those who rise as cream to the top of my milky memory. Chief among them are my editor friends at InterVarsity Press—Gary Deddo, Joel Scandrett, Jim Hoover (my hands-on-brain editor) and Ruth Goring (my hands-on-manuscript editor). The latter two have saved me from such embarrassment as you, dear readers, I hope never find out. Then there are two philosophers who read the manuscript in an early stage and helped immensely—Douglas Groothuis and Paul Chamberlain. Apologist, theologian and communications scholar Thomas Woodward read the chapter on evolution and has provided a critique found in the footnotes. None of them will want to be saddled with the approval of all my opinions, but all have my thanks for their helpful critique and suggestions for improvement.

Finally, I want to acknowledge the year-after-year commitment of my wife, who has provided both competent counsel when I have become too outrageous or reckless in my remarks and correction when I have simply been blind to my persistent carelessness with stylistic details, like spelling and punctuation, forsooth! Then, too, there are my children and grandchildren, the latter especially putting up with a lack of grandfatherly attention as I have had my mind preoccupied with the far less important matters of this book.

I trust that God, too, should be thanked for giving me all of what it has taken to write this and my other books. But I fear to embarrass him by suggesting that he is also responsible for the inadvertent errors and perhaps even chicanery of the books that have resulted. No, the responsibility for those stupidities and flummeries is all mine. Still, I can thank him for the unspeakable gift of his Son, our Lord Jesus Christ, for whose sake and in whose name go all these thanks to all of my helpers.

PREFACE

For years I have been arguing about the Christian faith privately with myself and publicly with others. And for the same number of years, I have experienced very slow going. Of course, my arguments have displayed all the elegance I could muster. I have delivered them in conversations and lectures with all the charisma I could display, capped with frequent humor redolent of Jay Leno and my fellow Nebraskan (I name-drop here) Johnny Carson. In fact, I have been rather impressed with my arguments. Nonetheless, they have rarely sparked the response I have really wanted—vast masses of friends and enemies flocking to Jesus to repent and say, "My Lord and my God!" Why is this?

I once asked a visiting philosopher/theologian from Britain to give me some insight. He had just lectured on postmodernism, arguing that much postmodern thought is self-referentially incoherent. In brief that means that if the case they make for their views leads to a true conclusion, it would contradict the premises on which their argument is based. This criticism of postmodernism has been made by many critics. But postmodern thinkers have not changed their minds. Why is this?

I am not the only Christian to experience such recalcitrance.[1] For example, in a public forum, when a pastor claimed that it should be obvious that child abuse is wrong, one woman responded: "What counts as abuse differs from society to society, so we can't really use the word *abuse* without tying it to a historical context." Even when challenged, she maintained her moral relativist stance. She could not see what I suspect most in the audience saw: such a view of morality is utterly bankrupt. The point here is, however, she did not change her mind—at least not then.

Why such refusal to see what most take as obvious? Two statements that contradict each other can't both be true. Child abuse is always wrong. Why don't some people see this?

I do not remember the British lecturer's exact words in response to my question, but their impact on me is easy to recall. Essentially he replied, "That's a stupid question. Anyone else have another question?"

That hurt. There in front of my friends, I had been shown out the door of rational discourse. Ah, yes, but by an utterly nonrational word from the podium. He had just used the logical fallacy of *name-calling*, sometimes called *poisoning the well* or *mud slinging* or *smoke and mirrors*. The technical term for the fallacy is *argumentum ad hominem*, that is, argument against the "man" (the arguer). In no way had the lecturer answered my question or addressed the issue.

The question itself still burns in my mind. Why aren't the presence and revelation of an obvious logical fallacy enough to disabuse a person from thinking his or her argument is worth accepting as true?

Recently I was asked to give several lectures and suggested this topic for one of them. I think it is well worth an answer. Why indeed don't solid, rational arguments for Christian faith usually persuade people to believe— even those people who claim to respect rationality? I proceeded to write and deliver this lecture. Though the audience did not flock to repent of their sins of irrationality, at least they did not stone me.

I now think I have enough to say on this subject to constitute a small book for people who wish to defend their Christian faith. The goal of the book is not only to help Christians deal with the seeming failure of their arguments but to help them construct more effective ways of presenting those arguments.

I have drawn liberally on my fifty-some years of experience arguing for the Christian faith. Some readers may, in fact, find themselves in the pages to follow. Not all my stories have happy endings. But I trust that readers will learn from my failures even more than I have.

So here I go again, constructing an argument—an argument about argument for arguers. Shall I have to deal with the failure of this argument as well? Let me know.

I BELIEVE—HELP MY UNBELIEF

A Credible Witness

This is a book about the way Christians can most effectively present a case for Christ. In short, it deals with the art of persuasion, the art of making the most credible witness to the truth of the Christian faith.

It is not so much a book filled with good arguments as one that examines the pitfalls facing Christians who wish not merely to assert the truth of the Christian faith but to do so with the greatest likelihood of success. I say *likelihood* because there are no surefire, knock-down arguments for anything a Christian believes. In fact, there are no surefire, knock-down arguments for anything anyone believes, even one who claims to believe nothing at all.

We human beings are finite in every way. We are born, live and die. We seem to know some things but often find out that what we thought we knew isn't true. We believe that our fundamental commitments to life are justifiable if not to others at least to us. Then we run smack up against a conundrum that shatters our self-satisfaction. At times we are like Alfred, Lord Tennyson after the death of his best friend:

Behold, we know not anything;
I can but trust that good shall fall
At last—far off—at last to all,
And every winter change to spring.

So runs my dream: but what am I?
An infant crying in the night,
An infant crying for the light,
And with no language but a cry.[1]

At other times we are like the man who said to Jesus, "I believe; help my unbelief!" (Mk 9:24). And at still other times we stand strong for our beliefs even when the evidence seems to go against them. We affirm, for example, the great goodness of God in the face of the tragedy of massive suffering.

Still, throughout all of our shilly-shallying, we know that we have duties. First, we must pass beyond being fed only the milk like babes in Christ; we must proceed to the meat of God's Word, developing confidence and grasping the strong reasons why it is not misplaced (Heb 5:12-14).

As maturing disciples of Christ, we have already been commissioned to spread the good news. Just before his departure from this earth, Jesus told his disciples, "All authority in heaven and on earth has been given to me." Then he drew a conclusion: "Go therefore and make disciples of all nations, baptizing them in the name of the Father and of the Son and of the Holy Spirit, and teaching them to obey everything that I have commanded you." And he followed it with a promise: "And remember, I am with you always, to the end of the age" (Mt 28:18-20).

Notice the "argument" that Jesus makes. He starts with an announcement that acts as the premise: I have all the authority in both heaven and earth. If that is so, then it follows logically that whatever he says should be obeyed.

What does he say? He says to his disciples, *Go.* Get out of here and spread the good news—*teach* everyone in the world what I have taught you. Make disciples so that they not only will know what I have taught but will, as a logical consequence, do what these teachings demand. Then, to let them know that they are not alone in this awesome task, he assures them of his presence. All we need as motivation and justification for our witness is right there in these words. They tell us what we are supposed to do, why we are supposed to do it and why the awesome task can be done.

Our job, then, is to be the best witnesses to Jesus Christ as Savior and Lord that we can be. It matters not the circumstances in which we find ourselves. This is clear from the words of the apostle Peter to believers who were being persecuted for their faith: "Always be ready to make your defense to anyone who demands from you an accounting for the hope that is in you; yet do it with gentleness and reverence. Keep your conscience clear, so that, when you are maligned, those who abuse you for your good conduct in Christ may be put to shame" (1 Pet 3:15-16).

Notice the words *defense* and *accounting*. What makes persuasive defense or good accounting? Essentially this:

A good case for the Christian faith lays before the watching world such a winsome embodiment of the Christian faith that for any and all who are willing to observe there will be an intellectually and emotionally credible witness to its fundamental truth.[2]

Elements from this brief description will crop up several times in the chapters to follow. This simple principle undergirds the argument of the present book.

In the process of practicing this approach to Christian witness, we will make many errors. Our "good" cases for the Christian faith will often not be so good. Our rejoinders to those who believe otherwise may miss the mark. Our attempts to be winsome will on occasion fall flat as we are perceived as arrogant or bigoted. And even our really good arguments, ones that should go a long way to persuading a seeker of the truth, will be misconstrued or just flat rejected.

No matter where we are on the scale of effective apologists, we all have a very long way to go. So let's get started.

Part one looks at the sorts of arguments that we are often tempted to use but that are so flawed that if we use them we should hang our head in shame. These are called "informal fallacies" by the professional logicians. Their ineptness and downright idiocy are aptly illustrated by a clever story by Max Shulman. I will use it as a takeoff point for a less humorous (sigh!) analysis.

Part two assumes that our arguments do not make any of these or any other fallacies but still prove ineffective. Why is this? What can we learn from the rejection our arguments often receive? Along the way, I trust that we will learn how we can make our arguments more effective, what arguments we may do well to stay away from even though they may be "good" ones from the standpoint of reason, and how taking the long way around may in the long run be the shortest way to opening closed minds to the good news.

Part three shifts to a positive mode, giving two examples of effective arguments—the ancient one presented by the apostle Paul in Athens and a recent one addressing a postmodern issue. Finally, an annotated bibliography listing further sources of arguments and rhetorical ploys forms the close.

PART ONE

COMMON LOGICAL FALLACIES

A good argument starts from true premises and/or facts, makes no logical mistakes (fallacies), marshals a great body of evidence, answers objections, clarifies the issues and draws valid (therefore true) conclusions. This is actually a very tall order, especially when an argument deals with profound theological or philosophical issues. Errors can be made at every point. Not all our premises are likely to be, strictly speaking, true. They may be ill-formed, fuzzy, close-but-no-cigar premises. Our facts may not be facts but misunderstandings. Our logic may be flawed.

In this section we will look at some very common logical fallacies, first by seeing them in a humorous setting, then in examples that, when one meets them in apologetic arguments, can be very painful. We need to see these fallacies from two perspectives—as those we encounter from our partners in dialogue and as those we may well be committing ourselves. But first a little instructive humor.

Max Shulman (1919-1988) was a popular writer who reflected on campus life in the 1950s. When I was an undergraduate at the University of Nebraska, I read his column regularly in the student newspaper. Later, when I was an English teacher, one of the texts I used to teach informal logic to first-year students was the story "Love Is a Fallacy." It comes from *The Many Loves of Dobie Gillis* (1951), and I am pleased to remind my fellow ancients of Shulman's wit and bring it to the attention of another generation of readers.[1]

---

[1]"Love Is a Fallacy" from *The Many Loves of Dobie Gillis*, ©1951, 1979 by Max Shulman is reprinted by permission of the Harold Matson Co., Inc.

"LOVE IS A FALLACY"

Max Shulman

Cool was I and logical. Keen, calculating, perspicacious, acute and astute—I was all of these. My brain was as powerful as a dynamo, as precise as a chemist's scales, as penetrating as a scalpel. And—think of it!—I was only eighteen.

It is not often that one so young has such a giant intellect. Take, for example, Petey Bellows, my roommate at the university. Same age, same background, but dumb as an ox. A nice enough fellow, you understand, but nothing upstairs. Emotional type. Unstable. Impressionable. Worst of all, a faddist. Fads, I submit, are the very negation of reason. To be swept up in every new craze that comes along, to surrender yourself to idiocy just because everybody else is doing it—this, to me, is the acme of mindlessness. Not, however, to Petey.

One afternoon I found Petey lying on his bed with an expression of such distress on his face that I immediately diagnosed appendicitis. "Don't move," I said. "Don't take a laxative. I'll get a doctor."

"Raccoon," he mumbled thickly.

"Raccoon?" I said, pausing in my flight.

"I want a raccoon coat," he wailed.

I perceived that his trouble was not physical, but mental. "Why do you want a raccoon coat?"

"I should have known it," he cried, pounding his temples. "I should have known they'd come back when the Charleston came back. Like a fool I spent all my money for textbooks, and now I can't get a raccoon coat."

"Can you mean," I said incredulously, "that people are actually wearing raccoon coats again?"

"All the Big Men on Campus are wearing them. Where've you been?"

"In the library," I said, naming a place not frequented by Big Men on Campus.

He leaped from the bed and paced the room. "I've got to have a raccoon coat," he said passionately. "I've got to!"

"Petey, why? Look at it rationally. Raccoon coats are unsanitary. They shed. They smell bad. They weigh too much. They're unsightly. They—"

"You don't understand," he interrupted impatiently. "It's the thing to do. Don't you want to be in the swim?"

"No," I said truthfully.

"Well, I do," he declared. "I'd give anything for a raccoon coat. Anything!"

My brain, that precision instrument, slipped into high gear. "Anything?" I asked, looking at him narrowly.

"Anything," he affirmed in ringing tones.

I stroked my chin thoughtfully. It so happened that I knew where to get my hands on a raccoon coat. My father had had one in his undergraduate days; it lay now in a trunk in the attic back home. It also happened that Petey had something I wanted. He didn't *have* it exactly, but at least he had first rights on it. I refer to his girl, Polly Espy.

I had long coveted Polly Espy. Let me emphasize that my desire for this young woman was not emotional in nature. She was, to be sure, a girl who excited the emotions, but I was not one to let my heart rule my head. I wanted Polly for a shrewdly calculated, entirely cerebral reason.

I was a freshman in law school. In a few years I would be out in practice. I was well aware of the importance of the right kind of wife in furthering a lawyer's career. The successful lawyers I had observed were, almost without exception, married to beautiful, gracious, intelligent women. With one omission, Polly fitted these specifications perfectly.

Beautiful she was. She was not yet of pin-up proportions, but I felt sure that time would supply the lack. She already had the makings.

Gracious she was. By gracious I mean full of graces. She had an erectness of carriage, an ease of bearing, a poise that clearly indicated the best of breeding. At table her manners were exquisite. I had seen her at the Kozy Kampus Korner eating the specialty of the house—a sandwich that contained scraps of pot roast, gravy, chopped nuts, and a dipper of sauerkraut—without even getting her fingers moist.

Intelligent she was not. In fact, she veered in the opposite direction. But I believed that under my guidance she would smarten up. At any rate, it was worth a try. It is, after all, easier to make a beautiful dumb girl smart than to make an ugly smart girl beautiful.

"Petey," I said, "are you in love with Polly Espy?"

"I think she's a keen kid," he replied, "but I don't know if you'd call it love. Why?"

"Do you," I asked, "have any kind of formal arrangement with her? I mean are you going steady or anything like that?"

"No. We see each other quite a bit, but we both have other dates. Why?"

"Is there," I asked, "any other man for whom she has a particular fondness?"

"Not that I know of. Why?"

I nodded with satisfaction. "In other words, if you were out of the picture, the field would be open. Is that right?"

"I guess so. What are you getting at?"

"Nothing, nothing," I said innocently, and took my suitcase out of the closet.

"Where are you going?" asked Petey.

"Home for the week end." I threw a few things into the bag.

"Listen," he said, clutching my arm eagerly, "while you're home, you couldn't get some money from your old man, could you, and lend it to me so I can buy a raccoon coat?"

"I may do better than that," I said with a mysterious wink and closed my bag and left.

"Look," I said to Petey when I got back Monday morning. I threw open the suitcase and revealed the huge, hairy, gamy object that my father had worn in his Stutz Bearcat in 1925.

"Holy Toledo!" said Petey reverently. He plunged his hands into the raccoon coat and then his face. "Holy Toledo!" he repeated fifteen or twenty times.

"Would you like it?" I asked.

"Oh yes!" he cried, clutching the greasy pelt to him. Then a canny look came into his eyes. "What do you want for it?"

"Your girl," I said, mincing no words.

"Polly?" he said in a horrified whisper. "You want Polly?"

"That's right."

He flung the coat from him. "Never," he said stoutly.

I shrugged. "Okay. If you don't want to be in the swim, I guess it's your business."

I sat down in a chair and pretended to read a book, but out of the corner of my eye I kept watching Petey. He was a torn man. First he looked at the coat with the expression of a waif at a bakery window. Then he turned away and set his jaw resolutely. Then he looked back at the coat, with even more longing in his face. Then he turned away, but with not so much resolution this time. Back and forth his head swiveled, desire waxing, resolution waning. Finally he didn't turn away at all; he just stood and stared with mad lust at the coat.

"It isn't as though I was in love with Polly," he said thickly. "Or going steady or anything like that."

"That's right," I murmured.

"What's Polly to me, or me to Polly?"

"Not a thing," said I.

"It's just been a casual kick—just a few laughs, that's all."

"Try on the coat," said I.

He complied. The coat bunched high over his ears and dropped all the way down to his shoe tops. He looked like a mound of dead raccoons. "Fits fine," he said happily.

I rose from my chair. "Is it a deal?" I asked, extending my hand.

He swallowed. "It's a deal," he said and shook my hand.

I had my first date with Polly the following evening. This was in the nature of a survey; I wanted to find out just how much work I had to do to get her mind up to the standard I required. I took her first to dinner. "Gee, that was a delish dinner," she said as we left the restaurant. Then I took her to a movie. "Gee, that was a marvy movie," she said as we left the theater. And then I took her home. "Gee, I had a sensaysh time," she said as she bade me good night.

I went back to my room with a heavy heart. I had gravely underestimated the size of my task. This girl's lack of information was terrifying. Nor would it be enough merely to supply her with information. First she had to be taught to *think*. This loomed as a project of no small dimensions, and at first I was tempted to give her back to Petey. But then I got to thinking about her abundant physical charms and about the way she entered a room and the way she handled a knife and fork, and I decided to make an effort.

I went about it, as in all things, systematically. I gave her a course in logic. It happened that I, as a law student, was taking a course in logic myself, so I had all the facts at my finger tips. "Polly," I said to her when I picked her up on our next date, "tonight we are going over to the Knoll and talk."

"Oo, terrif," she replied. One thing I will say for this girl: you would go far to find another so agreeable.

We went to the Knoll, the campus trysting place, and we sat down under an old oak, and she looked at me expectantly. "What are we going to talk about?" she asked.

"Logic."

She thought this over for a minute and decided she liked it. "Magnif," she said.

"Logic," I said, clearing my throat, "is the science of thinking. Before we can think correctly, we must first learn to recognize the common fallacies of logic. These we will take up tonight."

"Wow-dow!" she cried, clapping her hands delightedly.

I winced, but went bravely on. "First let us examine the fallacy called Dicto Simpliciter."

"By all means," she urged, batting her lashes eagerly.

"Dicto Simpliciter means an argument based on an unqualified generalization. For example: Exercise is good. Therefore everybody should exercise."

"I agree," said Polly earnestly. "I mean exercise is wonderful. I mean it builds the body and everything."

"Polly," I said gently, "the argument is a fallacy. *Exercise is good* is an unqualified generalization. For instance, if you have heart disease, exercise is bad, not good. Many people are ordered by their doctors *not* to exercise. You must *qualify* the generalization. You must say exercise is *usually* good, or exercise is good *for most people*. Otherwise you have committed a Dicto Simpliciter. Do you see?"

"No," she confessed. "But this is marvy. Do more! Do more!"

"It will be better if you stop tugging at my sleeve," I told her, and when she desisted, I continued. "Next we take up a fallacy called Hasty Generalization. Listen carefully: You can't speak French. I can't speak French. Petey Bellows can't speak French. I must therefore conclude that nobody at the University of Minnesota can speak French."

"Really?" said Polly, amazed. "*Nobody?*"

I hid my exasperation. "Polly, it's a fallacy. The generalization is reached too hastily. There are too few instances to support such a conclusion."

"Know any more fallacies?" she asked breathlessly. "This is more fun than dancing even."

I fought off a wave of despair. I was getting nowhere with this girl, absolutely nowhere. Still, I am nothing if not persistent. I continued. "Next comes Post Hoc. Listen to this: Let's not take Bill on our picnic. Every time we take him out with us, it rains."

"I know somebody just like that," she exclaimed. "A girl back home—Eula Becker, her name is. It never fails. Every single time we take her on a picnic—"

"Polly," I said sharply, "it's a fallacy. Eula Becker doesn't *cause* the rain. She has no connection with the rain. You are guilty of Post Hoc if you blame Eula Becker."

"I'll never do it again," she promised contritely. "Are you mad at me?"

I sighed. "No, Polly, I'm not mad."

"Then tell me some more fallacies."

"All right. Let's try Contradictory Premises."

"Yes, let's," she chirped, blinking her eyes happily.

I frowned, but plunged ahead. "Here's an example of Contradictory Premises: If God can do anything, can He make a stone so heavy that He won't be able to lift it?"

"Of course," she replied promptly.

"But if He can do anything, He can lift the stone," I pointed out.

"Yeah," she said thoughtfully. "Well, then I guess He can't make the stone."

"But He can do anything," I reminded her.

She scratched her pretty, empty head. "I'm all confused," she admitted.

"Of course you are. Because when the premises of an argument contradict each other, there can be no argument. If there is an irresistible force, there can be no immovable object. If there is an immovable object, there can be no irresistible force. Get it?"

"Tell me some more of this keen stuff," she said eagerly.

I consulted my watch. "I think we'd better call it a night. I'll take you home now, and you go over all the things you've learned. We'll have another session tomorrow night."

I deposited her at the girls' dormitory, where she assured me that she had had a perfectly terrif evening, and I went glumly home to my room. Petey lay snoring in his bed, the raccoon coat huddled like a great hairy beast at his feet. For a moment I considered waking him and telling him that he could have his girl back. It seemed clear that my project was doomed to failure. The girl simply had a logic-proof head.

But then I reconsidered. I had wasted one evening; I might as well waste another. Who knew? Maybe somewhere in the extinct crater of her mind a few embers still smoldered. Maybe somehow I could fan them into flame. Admittedly it was not a prospect fraught with hope, but I decided to give it one more try.

Seated under the oak the next evening I said, "Our first fallacy tonight is called Ad Misericordiam."

She quivered with delight.

"Listen closely," I said. "A man applies for a job. When the boss asks him what his qualifications are, he replies that he has a wife and six children at home, the wife is a helpless cripple, the children have nothing to eat, no clothes to wear, no shoes on their feet, there are no beds in the house, no coal in the cellar, and winter is coming."

A tear rolled down each of Polly's pink cheeks. "Oh, this is awful, awful," she sobbed.

"Yes, it's awful," I agreed, "but it's no argument. The man never answered the boss's question about his qualifications. Instead he appealed to the boss's sympathy. He committed the fallacy of Ad Misericordiam. Do you understand?"

"Have you got a handkerchief?" she blubbered.

I handed her a handkerchief and tried to keep from screaming while she wiped her eyes. "Next," I said in a carefully controlled tone, "we will discuss False Analogy. Here is an example: Students should be allowed to look at their textbooks during examinations. After all, surgeons have X rays to guide them during an operation, lawyers have briefs to guide them during a trial, carpenters have blueprints to guide them when they are building a house. Why, then, shouldn't students be allowed to look at their textbooks during an examination?"

"There now," she said enthusiastically, "is the most marvy idea I've heard in years."

"Polly," I said testily, "the argument is all wrong. Doctors, lawyers, and carpenters aren't taking a test to see how much they have learned, but students are. The situations are altogether different, and you can't make an analogy between them."

"I still think it's a good idea," said Polly.

"Nuts," I muttered. Doggedly I pressed on. "Next we'll try Hypothesis Contrary to Fact."

"Sounds yummy," was Polly's reaction.

"Listen: If Madame Curie had not happened to leave a photographic plate in a drawer with a chunk of pitchblende, the world today would not know about radium."

"True, true," said Polly, nodding her head. "Did you see the movie? Oh, it just knocked me out. That Walter Pidgeon is so dreamy. I mean he fractures me."

"If you can forget Mr. Pidgeon for a moment," I said coldly, "I would like to point out that the statement is a fallacy. Maybe Madame Curie would have discovered radium at some later date. Maybe somebody else would have discovered it. Maybe any number of things would have happened. You can't start with a hypothesis that is not true and then draw any supportable conclusions from it."

"They ought to put Walter Pidgeon in more pictures," said Polly. "I hardly ever see him any more."

One more chance, I decided. But just one more. There is a limit to what flesh and blood can bear. "The next fallacy is called Poisoning the Well."

"How cute!" she gurgled.

"Two men are having a debate. The first one gets up and says, 'My opponent is a notorious liar. You can't believe a word that he is going to say.' . . . Now, Polly, think. Think hard. What's wrong?"

I watched her closely as she knit her creamy brow in concentration. Suddenly a glimmer of intelligence—the first I had seen—came into her eyes. "It's not fair," she said with indignation. "It's not a bit fair. What chance has the second man got if the first man calls him a liar before he even begins talking?"

"Right!" I cried exultantly. "One hundred per cent right. It's not fair. The first man has *poisoned the well* before anybody could drink from it. He has hamstrung his opponent before he could even start. . . . Polly, I'm proud of you."

"Pshaw," she murmured, blushing with pleasure.

"You see, my dear, these things aren't so hard. All you have to do is concentrate. Think—examine—evaluate. Come now, let's review everything we have learned."

"Fire away," she said with an airy wave of her hand.

Heartened by the knowledge that Polly was not altogether a cretin, I began a long, patient review of all I had told her. Over and over and over again I cited instances, pointed out flaws, kept hammering away without letup. It was like digging a tunnel. At first everything was work, sweat, and darkness. I had no idea when I would reach the light, or even *if* I would. But I persisted. I pounded and clawed and scraped, and finally I was rewarded. I saw a chink of light. And then the chink got bigger and the sun came pouring in and all was bright.

Five grueling nights this took, but it was worth it. I had made a logician out of Polly; I had taught her to think. My job was done. She was worthy of me at last. She was a fit wife for me, a proper hostess for my many mansions, a suitable mother for my well-heeled children.

It must not be thought that I was without love for this girl. Quite the contrary. Just as Pygmalion loved the perfect woman he had fashioned, so I loved mine. I decided to acquaint her with my feelings at our very next meeting. The time had come to change our relationship from academic to romantic.

"Polly," I said when next we sat beneath our oak, "tonight we will not discuss fallacies."

"Aw, gee," she said, disappointed.

"My dear," I said, favoring her with a smile, "we have now spent five evenings together. We have gotten along splendidly. It is clear that we are well-matched."

"Hasty Generalization," said Polly brightly.

"I beg your pardon," said I.

"Hasty Generalization," she repeated. "How can you say that we are well matched on the basis of only five dates?"

I chuckled with amusement. The dear child had learned her lessons well. "My dear," I said, patting her hand in a tolerant manner, "five dates is plenty. After all, you don't have to eat a whole cake to know that it's good."

"False Analogy," said Polly promptly. "I'm not a cake. I'm a girl."

I chuckled with somewhat less amusement. The dear child had learned her lessons perhaps too well. I decided to change tactics. Obviously the best approach was a simple, strong, direct declaration of love. I paused for a moment while my massive brain chose the proper words. Then I began:

"Polly, I love you. You are the whole world to me, and the moon and the stars and the constellations of outer space. Please, my darling, say that you will go steady with me, for if you will not, life will be meaningless. I will languish. I will refuse my meals. I will wander the face of the earth, a shambling, hollow-eyed hulk."

There, I thought, folding my arms, that ought to do it.

"Ad Misericordiam," said Polly.

I ground my teeth. I was not Pygmalion; I was Frankenstein, and my monster had me by the throat. Frantically I fought back the tide of panic surging through me. At all costs I had to keep cool.

"Well, Polly," I said, forcing a smile, "you certainly have learned your fallacies."

"You're darn right," she said with a vigorous nod.

"And who taught them to you, Polly?"

"You did."

"That's right. So you do owe me something, don't you, my dear? If I hadn't come along you never would have learned about fallacies."

"Hypothesis Contrary to Fact," she said instantly.

I dashed perspiration from my brow. "Polly," I croaked, "you mustn't take all these things so literally. I mean this is just classroom stuff. You know that the things you learn in school don't have anything to do with life."

"Dicto Simpliciter," she said, wagging her finger at me playfully.

That did it. I leaped to my feet, bellowing like a bull. "Will you or will you not go steady with me?"

"I will not," she replied.

"Why not?" I demanded.

"Because this afternoon I promised Petey Bellows that I would go steady with him."

I reeled back, overcome with the infamy of it. After he promised, after he made a deal, after he shook my hand! "The rat!" I shrieked, kicking up great chunks of turf. "You can't go with him, Polly. He's a liar. He's a cheat. He's a rat."

"Poisoning the Well," said Polly, "and stop shouting. I think shouting must be a fallacy too."

With an immense effort of will, I modulated my voice. "All right," I said. "You're a logician. Let's look at this thing logically. How could you choose Petey Bellows over me? Look at me—a brilliant student, a tremendous intellectual, a man with an assured future. Look at Petey—a knothead, a jitterbug, a guy who'll never know where his next meal is coming from. Can you give me one logical reason why you should go steady with Petey Bellows?"

"I certainly can," declared Polly. "He's got a raccoon coat."

YOU'RE ALL HYPOCRITES!

Unqualified and Hasty Generalizations

Dobie Gillis was not so "keen, calculating, perspicacious, acute and astute" as he thought, was he? Not surprising, since he was so confident that he was all these and more! Arrogance, aggression and cleverness—as well as shouting—could also be labeled as fallacies. And, indeed, we will consider them in due time.

Here, however, let's begin with the logical fallacies Shulman has identified. We meet them in two ways: (1) when we use them unwittingly and get caught by our audience and (2) when our dialogue partners spring them on us as objections to our argument. In both cases we need to keep our wits about us, admit when we've been unfair and be gentle when we point out the errors of others.

UNQUALIFIED GENERALIZATIONS: DICTO SIMPLICITER

There is little that upsets me in dialogues with friends who disagree with my religious positions as much as the often-but-not-always-true generalizations that pop up. Statements like this occur with regularity:

> *"Biblical scholars say the Gospels were written long after the events they record and are distorted by the viewpoint of the author and the need for the accounts to address the situation of the early church."*

What follows from this half-truth is the conclusion that today we cannot trust the Gospels to relate the events of Jesus' life accurately. Therefore, any particular point I am trying to make from a given passage is considered dubious at best and false at worst. Stated in this manner, it relativizes all New Testament theology. We do not have an authoritative text from which we can build a understanding of Jesus as Jesus really was, only an understanding that combines the perspective of the Gospel writer and his audience.

If I am to counter this *dicto simpliciter*, I have to challenge the premise on several counts:

1. While some scholars make such a statement, not *all* qualified scholars do so; here I might mention some who take a different, more conservative approach (see, for example, the annotated bibliography, pp. 161-63).

2. Neither the viewpoint of the Gospel author nor the needs of the audience necessarily distort the Gospel text.[1]

3. Unless there is a parallel in one of the other Gospels, there is usually no other viewpoint available to us. That is, if we are to know anything at all about the issues mentioned, this is all we have to go on, which means we have no way of assessing how much (or even whether) it is a distortion of the truth. In fact, if we do believe that the text has distorted reality, it is probably because we are approaching it with a predetermined notion of what could possibly happen. For example, miracles can't happen; therefore the stories of miracles are distortions of the truth.

4. The church has been trusting the four Gospels to lead them to the truth about God for two thousand years. It is only chronological snobbery—we moderns know more about everything than the ancients—that justifies our assumption of interpretative superiority.

What a task! Can I actually get away with making this response? Of course I can do so when I am asked such a question in a public forum and I have the microphone. But if it's a casual comment around a table at Starbucks, it's hard to command enough attention to get out such a long response. Still, I try to get a little out.

Here's another one that comes up frequently:

"The Bible is full of contradictions. We can't trust it to tell the truth."

I may well want to treat this first statement as a false premise. As it stands, it is. But it is a common comment, and if my response is "No, the Bible is not full of contradictions," it will simply pit my authority against that of the one asking the question. The asker—and the audience, if this is a public arena—will have little basis on which to decide between us.

Better to say, "Oh, really? I don't think so. But which contradictions did you have in mind?"

Usually, the asker doesn't have any in mind. If he or she does, I may address one or two of them individually, then say, "We can talk afterward about others you are concerned about." This demonstrates that for the most part the objection is without real merit, and the dialogue can turn elsewhere.

Of course, one should be clear about just what constitutes a contradiction. A genuine contradiction occurs only when some specific thing is both asserted and denied. Most alleged biblical contradictions are not of this type. Rather, the contradictions tend to be between a reader's interpretation of one text and his or her interpretation of another text. The proper solution may be to point out that these contradictions may be only apparent; because of the different contexts of the two texts, they may not actually be affirming and denying the same thing.

If the objector raises an apparent contradiction that I can't handle, I can admit that I don't have enough information to respond at the moment but promise to get a response to the objector by e-mail. I don't remember ever having to do that. This is not because I am so knowledgeable but because the alleged contradictions most people know about are easily addressed (see the bibliography, pp. 161-63).

Christians, too, make unqualified generalizations, about matters of Christian faith, about other religions and their adherents. Here are a few examples:

"Muslims believe in holy war. We will never find a way to live together in peace."

"Christians are a peaceful people."

"Christians understand the truth about God."

"The Bible clearly states the doctrine of the Trinity."

"Christians believe in the truth; Buddhists don't."

Each of these statements contains a grain of truth, but they are so unqualified that they almost succeed in being false. We need to guard against making claims like these. They weaken our credibility and end up belying the truth.

HASTY GENERALIZATION

Sometimes objectors to the Christian faith will lump all Christians together, accusing the many of the sins of the few. Here are four illustrations:

"Televangelists are just out for your money. Look at how they all beg for funds, then live in luxury. Look at Jim and Tammy Faye Bakker."

"You Christians are hypocrites. You accuse others of the sins you yourselves commit. Look at Jimmy Swaggart."

"Wars are the result of religious controversy. It would be better if religion disappeared completely."

"Look at all the priests who have abused children. If church leaders can't live like they're supposed to, why should I think their religion is worth considering?"

These sentiments are common, but it is not difficult to show that they are not universally true. Often they express a generalized frustration based in part on prejudice or on personal experience of Christians' genuine failure to live up to high biblical standards. We Christians rarely live as Jesus commanded. But Jesus did. And it is Jesus who justifies the truth of the Christian faith—not us.

There is, of course, no reason for one who is speaking up for the faith to defend the indefensible. Some television evangelists do seem to be at fault. But not all. Thankfully, we can point to Billy Graham as one model of how Christians should behave.

Religious passions have been a factor in some wars. When the conflicts are looked at closely, other factors like economics and political power are even more important. Others, like World War II, are not so much about religion as they are about attempting to uphold more universal ethical standards. Moreover, war often brings out compassionate Christian responses to those on both sides who suffer its consequences.

Here are a few more comments from people who have been put off by their own experiences:

"I've tried to read the Bible, but I can't make heads or tails of it."

"I went to church once, but I couldn't get much out of it."

"I used to go to church, but people were just plain unfriendly or rude."

"They do weird things in church. I'm confused. I never know when I'm supposed to kneel or stand. And what is that motion people make with their hands when they try to find a seat?"

Most comments like these betray hasty generalizations. They can be countered by information that qualifies them so much that the objector comes to realize that the grain of truth they contain is just that—a grain. It is easy for us simply to invite the objector to our own church and to read Scripture together. The objector may well have begun in Genesis and soon become baffled. Invite them to read one of the Gospels. Mark and Luke are especially good for first-time Gospel readers.

Again, we Christians ourselves are often guilty of hasty generalizations. For example:

> *"Non-Christians just don't understand what they are rejecting."*
>
> *"If you're not a Christian, you have no reason for being good."*
>
> *"I went to a Buddhist monastery, and all I heard was a buzz from the meditation. Buddhists have blown their minds."*
>
> *"Church is a wonderful place."*
>
> *"Christians are so loving."*

When we make these sorts of statements, we should expect to be challenged. We had better be prepared to qualify and justify them or not make them at all.

INDUCTIVE ARGUMENTS

Unqualified and hasty generalizations are fallacies associated with *inductive arguments*. Many, if not most, of the arguments used to defend the Christian faith are inductive. That is, they begin with evidence and move toward a generalization. For example,

> *In John 14:6-7, Jesus said, "I am the way, and the truth, and the life. No one comes to the Father except through me. If you know me, you will know my Father also."*
>
> *Therefore, Jesus was making a claim to be God (or at least to have divine status).*

This is a generalization based on a fairly straightforward understanding of these words of Jesus. Is it hasty? Maybe. For one thing, it assumes without demonstration that Jesus actually said words in his own language that have been transmitted faithfully and translated into concepts that we have correctly understood. A good argument for this assumption is long and complicated and assumes a host of further notions.

Let's say that we find in the Gospels a second remark by Jesus that seems to make a claim to deity. Then a third and a fourth. What if we found fifty such sentences? How many are enough to avoid the charge of hasty generalization? There is no rule. There is only increasing probability. All arguments from facts (data, evidence) to conclusions are *probable;* therefore, they can be said to be problematic. Indeed, eminent philosopher Alfred North Whitehead called inductive arguments "the despair of philosophy."[2]

Nonetheless, inductive arguments are the staple form of argument in every realm, from daily life (why is the roof leaking?) to crime investigation (who done it?), historical research (did Caesar cross the Rubicon?) and scientific theories (including evolution). Aristotle recognized this when he said. "It is a sign of an uneducated person to require more evidence than that thing was capable of providing."[3] The point here is that many arguments in defense of Christian faith are inductive arguments, and the best that can be gained from them is probability. Assessing that probability is a highly subjective matter. As we will see below, there seems to be no amount of evidence that can be amassed against the naturalistic theory of evolution to lessen its hold on the minds of many scientists.

As those who seek to make effective arguments, therefore, we should be aware of the potential weakness of generalizations—our own and those of people we are trying to persuade. Acknowledging that rational conclusions are often based on judgments that go beyond the evidence will help us respect the judgments of those who disagree with us without letting their judgments sway our own. It also rightly forces us to draw together as many evidences (or as many reasons) as we can for the position we are defending.

IT'S DANGEROUS TO BELIEVE YOU'RE RIGHT

Causes and Contradictions

Causes are notoriously hard to determine. David Hume, in fact, argued that if all we have to work from are the impressions our mind receives, the very reality of cause itself is suspect. He acknowledged, however, that we constantly use this concept even if we can't be sure it labels anything in reality. Immanuel Kant thought that the notion of cause and effect is a *category,* a pretheoretical given—a tool we use and must use whether we understand its foundation or not.[1]

Whatever is the explanation for our notion of cause and effect, we constantly think and live by its terms. We may not, like Polly Espy, believe that Eula Becker causes the rain on our picnic, but we think something did. In fact we think or act as if every event has a cause. Cause is especially relevant when we examine why we believe and act as we do. When it comes to spiritual matters, the stakes are high indeed. "What must I do to inherit eternal life?" the rich man asked Jesus (Mk 10:17). Understanding the answer Jesus gave is still vital for us.

FALSE CAUSE: POST HOC AND OTHER CAUSAL FALLACIES

The fallacy of *false cause* is a constant bugbear in Christian witness. Sometimes we fall into it with the best of intent and some truth. Take this common comment a Christian might well make while speaking in favor of Christian faith:

"Last week Joe committed his life to Christ. He's been a changed man ever since."

The implication is that Joe's faith has caused the change in his life. Most evangelical Christians will find nothing at all suspect in this conclusion. Because of their background beliefs and experience, it's an easy conclusion for Christians to accept. Christians know that this sort of transformation does take place. But saying this about Joe will probably not impress an audience that has never heard of Joe before. If they have known others who have had a significant life change following their commitment to Christ, it may carry some weight. But without some former experience of transformation following Christian conversion, or if those we are speaking to neither know Joe nor have seen the change, there may be little merit in using the statement as a justification for Christian faith.

On the other hand, the biographies of well-known Christians can make a strong and reasonable case for the Christian faith. The life stories of people like Joni Eareckson Tada, C. S. Lewis, St. Augustine, Corrie ten Boom, Charles Colson, Aleksandr Solzhenitsyn and hosts of others make a distinct contribution.

Unfortunately, in Christian literature and witness, too many statements made have multiple major problems. They are too simplistic, claim too much and can easily be countered by contrary experiences and illustrations. To mention a few:

"America has become a powerful nation because it is founded on Christian principles."

This is highly dubious. Any serious, nonbiased study of American history will show that there were a host of factors involved in America's rise to power and some of them were counter to Christian belief. Moreover, America was founded as much on Enlightenment deism as on fully Christian principles. It does us no good to make claims that can be legitimately challenged by those with knowledge of our checkered past, let alone our more obvious tarnished present.

"Since I became a Christian I have been employed throughout the entire economic turndown of the past five years."

The implication that one's Christian faith caused full employment is easily countered by Christians like my own son, who was out of a job for over a year. Richard's testimony is that God sustained his family as he and his wife took up temporary jobs, relied on unemployment compensation for the first six months and received help from generous neighbors and friends. As I first drafted this, he was again out of work; as I revise it he has found an excellent steady job (but for how long?). Cautious, realistic stories of God's sustaining grace during trials—illness, death of loved ones, wars and rumors of wars—are more effective. And they go deeper into the character of the God in whom we trust.

We turn now to an illustration of false cause that turns out to be part of a convoluted series of fallacies. The illustration has both the virtue of being an actual argument published in a leading American newspaper and the vice of being somewhat complex. In any case, examining it can help us see how subtle but misleading arguments can be untwisted through careful reading and good thinking.

A particularly egregious statement was made by Jerry Falwell after the tragedy of 9/11. Whatever the context in which he made the comment, it was picked up by the secular media and thrown in the face of Christians. First the comment:

I really believe that the pagans, and the abortionists, and the feminists, and the gays and lesbians who are actively trying to make that an alternative lifestyle, the A.C.L.U., People for the American Way—all of them have tried to secularize America—I point the finger in their face and say, "You helped this happen."[2]

Unless God has appointed Falwell as a prophet, there is no justification for his saying this in public or perhaps even at all. Without analysis or argument, his statement assigns a significant amount of *cause*—thus guilt—to particular groups of people Falwell believes are promoting false values. For a moment, let us say he is correct—insensitive (for which he has apologized) but correct.

First, there is a rhetorical problem. What possible weight will his proclamation carry with the people he has accused? Its offense will help solidify their commitment to false values.

Second, is the problem of showing that this claim is true. What evidence can Falwell cite—the Bible? Not only do the accused reject it as a moral authority, but Falwell has to have had a specific hermeneutic and resulting theology to reach this conclusion. That perspective is limited to a fairly narrow band of American Christians, so narrow that other Christian commentators were quick to distance themselves from Falwell's remark.

Third, Falwell missed an opportunity to consider that his own Christian theology and practices might have been among the causes of 9/11. In any case, it is highly unlikely that bin Laden had abortionists or homosexual communities in mind. It is more likely that he had in mind those who were supporting Israel in the Palestinian conflict—in other words, the Christian political right, perhaps Falwell himself. (If I were to claim this possibility as a reality, however, I too would be guilty of false cause.)

But look at the issue. What did God have in mind? Did God use bin Laden as he used Cyrus to accomplish his purpose (Is 45:1-4)? For which of our many sins were we Americans being punished? We can speculate. We can examine our own possible role in creating an America that is hateful to many people in other countries—not just Muslims. That would be a more proper response. Still, the question remains: how can we know God's intentions in any specific current historic event?

If Falwell's apologetic faux pas were not enough, look at how Andrew Sullivan used it in his *New York Times Magazine* article "This Is a Religious War." His article is equally flawed by the *post hoc ergo propter hoc* (after this, therefore because of this) fallacy. This time the fallacy is used against Falwellian fundamentalism.

> *The critical link between Western and Middle Eastern fundamentalism is surely the pace of social change. If you take your beliefs from books written more than a thousand years ago, and you believe in these texts literally, then the appearance of the modern world must truly terrify. If you believe that women should be assigned to polygamous, concealed servitude, then Manhattan must appear like Gomorrah. If you believe that homosexuality is a crime punishable by death, as both fundamental Islam and the Bible dictate, then a world of same-sex marriage is surely Sodom. It is not a big step to argue that such centers of evil should be destroyed or undermined, as bin Laden does, or to believe that their destruction is somehow a consequence of their sin, as Jerry Falwell argued.*[3]

There are enough fallacies in these five sentences to choke this present analysis. But let's take a few. The opening sentence is, of course, dubious (are American fundamentalists afraid of change or the pace of change, or are they discouraged by the *direction* of that change?), but let it stand for the moment. It's the second sentence that is loaded with unstated assumptions. First, it assumes that books written over a thousand years ago contain only propositions or moral positions that are no longer valid. That can't be so or "You shall not murder" and "You shall not lie" would now be invalid.

Second, Sullivan distorts the New Testament teaching. Perhaps the Qur'an does call for the death of homosexuals; certainly the Old Testament did so for those who committed homosexual acts (Lev 20:13). But Jesus is not recorded as saying anything at all about the homosexual condition, let alone affirming the death penalty for its practice. And while Paul rejects the propriety of homosexual acts, he says nothing about punishment. Moreover, Jesus rejected the death penalty for multiple adultery (Lev 20:10; Jn 8:2-11); might he not also have done so for homosexual acts? I know of no American fundamentalists who believe in the death penalty for practicing homosexuals, let alone for those with homosexual tendencies who live celibate lives.

Third, even if fundamentalists actually hold to an "ancient" creed, they are by no means necessarily terrified by the modern world as Sullivan says. To say so is *dicto simpliciter* (an unqualified generalization; see above, pp. 33-36). Nor are they necessarily predisposed to violence. Actually, Sullivan admits this when he says, "Mercifully, violence has not been a significant feature of this [fundamentalist] trend [linking religion with politics]."[4]

Fourth, the main fallacy is to find the cause leading to 9/11 not to be a particular strain of fundamentalist Islam but to be a more general (and amorphous) religious attitude called fundamentalism, and then to say that Western fundamentalism is (or will become) therefore just as much a cause of acts of terror like 9/11 as one strain of Islamic fundamentalism. His definition of *fundamentalism* is especially troubling. Fundamentalism, he says, is "the blind recourse to texts embraced as literal truth, the injunction to follow the commandments of God before anything else, the subjugation of reason and judgment and even conscience to the dictates of dogma."[5]

This definition is a frustrating caricature of the faith of the bulk of people in the United States who are happy to be called or call themselves fundamentalists. First, it is filled with language loaded with negative connotations: *blind*, *literal truth*, *dictates* and *dogma*. Rhetoricians sometimes call these *stigma-words*. They amount to name-calling (see pp. 62-67 below).

Second, not only fundamentalists but all traditional Christians believe in following the commandments of God before anything else.

Third, all traditional Christians affirm the Bible as the source of their beliefs. But even among extreme fundamentalists, only a few do so blindly. I think Sullivan might be shocked to see just how intellectually sophisticated the theologies of the fundamentalists really are, or at least can be.

Fifth, accepting the Bible as literal truth—as fundamentalists may well do—does not mean reading it unintelligently; it means reading it *as it was written* (literally), that is, in such a way that one gets the meanings that the biblical authors intended. If one wants an illustration of reading the Bible as it was *not* intended to be read, look at the work of the Jesus Seminar.

Sixth, dogma is not formulated so that reason and judgment have to be subjected to it; it has been formulated by Christian scholars using the best reason and judgment they could muster. To acknowledge that an ancient document—say the Nicene Creed—is authoritative for Christian belief can be highly rational.

Sullivan then turns to what some call the fallacy of the *slippery slope*. He writes that fundamentalist commitments can be

> *exhilarating and transformative. They [fundamentalist commitments] have led human beings to perform extraordinary acts of both good and evil. And they have an internal logic to them. If you believe that there is an eternal afterlife and the endless indescribable torture awaits those who disobey God's law, then it requires no huge stretch of imagination to make sure that you not only conform to each dictate but that you encourage and, if neces-sary, coerce others to do the same. The logic behind this is impeccable. . . . In a world of absolute truth, in matters graver than life and death, there is no room for dissent and no room for theological doubt. Hence the reliance on literal interpretations of texts—because interpretation can lead to error and error can lead to damnation.[6]*

The argument Sullivan outlines is not impeccable, nor is it one used by so-called fundamentalists. Rather, it is an *ad hominem* comment fabricated by Sullivan (it was used by the Inquisition in the Middle Ages, but I know no fundamentalists who coerce belief by threats of violence), and as noted, it is an illustration of the slippery slope fallacy. For example, some teetotalers say, "If you take one drink and like it, you will take many drinks and become an alcoholic." This is simply not true. The slope is not that slippery. It is just such slippery slope thinking that characterizes Sullivan's argument that if you believe you are absolutely right about the future of those who do not believe that no one comes to the Father but by Jesus, you will use force to coerce belief. Such use of force, however, has always been an aberration of Jesus' teaching and a travesty of his example. Jesus died for his belief that he was the Messiah; he did not kill for it, nor did he command his disciples to do so. Even bin Laden's terrorists did not kill people in the World Trade Center to coerce belief. Their actions may have had more to do with assuring paradise for themselves and making a moral and political statement for a particular strain of Islam.

What Sullivan has done is to forget that the danger does not come from the tenacious character of a person's belief that he or she is right but from the content of that belief. Quakers believe absolutely in nonviolence. Violence is the last thing that such an absolutist belief will encourage. But one need not go to the pacifists among Christians. Just war theology—if held tenaciously as absolutely true and practiced by the bulk of governments— would prevent most if not all wars.

A month after Sullivan's piece, Thomas L. Friedman wrote an op-ed article for the *New York Times*.[7] He too argued that we are not fighting terrorism but "religious totalitarianism," a prime facet of which is "preaching exclusivist religious visions." We ought to promote "an ideology of pluralism—an ideology that embraces religious diversity and the idea that my faith can be nurtured without claiming exclusive truth." That is, we should have "a multilingual view of God—a notion that God is not exhausted by just one religious path."

Two days later David Shnaider replied in a letter to the *Times:*

> How is Thomas L. Friedman's assertion that religions must give up any claim to "exclusive truth" not just another version of the religious totalitarianism that he opposes so strongly? . . . The essence of Judaism, Christianity, Islam, Mormonism and many other faiths is that each represents the true

path to salvation. This is not fundamentalism, but the teaching of the prophets and apostles.

Modern Western civilization is testimony to the idea that it is possible to believe in an exclusive truth, as many observant believers do, without preaching, as the Taliban did, that no other beliefs can be tolerated.[8]

I couldn't have said it better myself. Shnaider's critique of Friedman serves as well for Sullivan. Sullivan's and Friedman's religious pluralism is in fact self-referentially incoherent. (See also the critique of religious pluralism on pp. 109-13, 146-55 and 170-73 below.)

Sullivan's extended argument and Friedman's simple reduction illustrate the sorts of complex and convoluted arguments serious Christians face. Sloppy thinking in pursuit of justifying an ideology is always a temptation, and the resulting sin is evident in the most supposedly responsible publications by the most sophisticated analysts and pundits. *Caveat emptor* (let the buyer beware) is a warning for buyers; *lector emptor* goes for readers, even of the *New York Times*. In fact, *lector emptor* goes as well for readers of both Christians and their critics.

CAUSES AND REASONS

Causes and reasons are often confused with one another. A distinction between them, however, is important. Let's say you ask a group of students this question: "Why do you—or people in general—believe what you or they do?" The answer always includes statements like these: "My parents are Christians," "I grew up going to church," "My parents never believed in God, and neither do I," or, from one raised in a communist bloc country, "I was taught that God was a myth, that Jesus Christ did not even exist."

These factors leading to specific religious or nonreligious belief are not really reasons; they are *causes*. Nothing explicitly rational was involved. Children raised in Poona, India, by Hindu parents will inevitably grow up with some form of Hindu belief. Only if they encounter another belief system, say at school with Muslims or Christians, will they be anything other than basically Hindu in their worldview. They have been *caused* to believe what they believe. Their beliefs have been formed by sociological forces. That does not mean that their beliefs are not genuinely intellectual, that they are something less than rationally justifiable, only that they have not been formed primarily by thinking through various options, responding to possible objections and arriving at consciously rational conclusions.[9]

The question "Why do you believe what you do?" also has a host of other answers, such as, "My belief in God gives me hope," "My faith provides meaning and direction for my life," "The Scriptures tell me who God is and how I can get to know him," "There is a lot of evidence that Jesus was and is the Son of God" or "The Christian worldview provides the best explanation for all the tough questions I have about life." These and many other similar responses are *reasons*. Whether weak or strong, based on the truth or not, they involve the application of the mind to the matter of belief.

Why is the distinction between causes and reasons important? There are at least two reasons. First, if the people I am addressing are largely young and have not reflected on the reasons for their belief, I want to help them become conscious of their lack of conscious rational foundation (that is, lack of reasons) for their orientation to life. I see this as important for everyone, both Christians and others. It is important for Christians because without some sense of why they are Christians, they may well hold their faith with reservations (and thus weaken their Christian life) or lose their faith entirely. In my experience, many Christians simply cannot give a "reason for the hope that is within them." For those who are not Christians, distinguishing between causes and reasons is important because it removes a barrier to belief and opens the way for them to see the credibility of the Christian faith.

Second, the distinction is important because one of the charges against Christians is that they believe what they do primarily—or solely—because they have been raised in a Christian environment. They have been *caused* to believe. If they thought about it, skeptics say, they would change their minds. Some atheist professors make it their goal to destroy the Christian faith of their students. Their task is much easier with those students whose faith has been acquired in a relatively sequestered environment and thus is largely the same as that of their parents or their friends. Students who have gone through crises of belief or conversion are often stronger and more able to resist the pressure from a hostile environment shaped by an atheist intent on destroying Christian faith. The point here, however, is that when one hears a sociology professor say that religious beliefs are formed solely or even primarily by social factors (and thus are *caused*), it is a form of *post hoc* fallacy.

If it is true that religious beliefs are formed *solely* by sociological causes (the religious environment), then there is at least a strong possibility that sociological theories were formed in the same way (the academic environment of professional sociology). Sociological theories would then have no more likelihood of being true than religious convictions.

The same is true of the basically Freudian thesis that belief in God and religion in general is a form of wish fulfillment and therefore an illusion. When this objection arises in popular discourse, it is easily countered in several ways.[10] First, if belief in God is a product of wish fulfillment for those who believe, atheism (utter nonbelief in any supernatural) is just as likely to be a product of the same kind. People who do not believe in God often do so because it relieves them from feeling guilty about how they are living their lives. They see the Christian God as a stern judge, not a God to be wished.

This leads to the second rejoinder. The Christian God is not a God anyone would at first wish for, not because of his vindictive character but because he demands total surrender. "Those who try to make their life secure will lose it," Jesus said, "but those who lose their life will keep it" (Lk 17:33). Salvation, which on the one hand is utterly a gift of God, comes at a very high price. The very exclusiveness of Christian faith—"I am the way, and the truth, and the life" (Jn 14:6)—carries a stigma in our pluralist society. It is, of course, true that the hard truth of the Christian faith involves the greatest of all benefits—life with God and his forever family—and that is an end greatly to be desired. It is just not a benefit that is likely to be understood well enough to be wished by one who is not already a believer.

But the fact that we have a prior desire for the existence of God who would be a perfect Father does not mean that this desire causes our belief. There is a truth in Freud's analysis: As Christians we can agree that we have a desire for God, a primal, unfulfilled pretheoretical longing for significance and meaning. God has "set eternity in the hearts of men; yet they cannot fathom what God has done from beginning to end" (Eccles 3:11 NIV). There really is a God who is there, One who alone satisfies this longing. "Our hearts are restless till they rest in thee," said St. Augustine.[11] And John Calvin talked about a *sensus divinitas* (a "direct sense of the divine").[12] We long for God because he wants us to. Belief in his existence does not follow from our desire; his existence triggers our desire.

If belief in God is a result of wish fulfillment, then it is just as likely that nonbelief in God is a result of wish fulfillment. The believer wants to believe in God; the nonbeliever doesn't want to believe in God. The argument about whether God exists is a draw. Neither side makes a case.

There is a general principle involved: Nonrational causes of any kind—sociological, psychological, anthropological—cut both ways. If one side attributes the other view to emotion, ulterior motive, cultural formation or psychological need, then the other side needs only to reply in kind.[13] For example, one Christian critic of evolution writes this:

> *In short, acceptance by the public of the truth of unintelligent evolution [i.e., naturalistic evolution] gives to scientists a greater share of power, prestige, and income that otherwise would go to the religious. The success of the scientific establishment in this debate has enabled it to humiliate the religious and drive them from the podium from which truths about the physical world are pronounced.[14]*

What he says may well be true. But it is not—or ought not be—an effective argument. All the evolutionist needs to do in response is charge the anti-evolutionist with envying the power that the evolutionists now have.

Christians can stay away from at least some fruitless arguments by avoiding attributing nonrational causes to the beliefs of their opponents. Such arguments are too easily turned on their heads and used legitimately against Christians.

CONTRARY HYPOTHESES

God is omnipotent. So is he so strong that he can make a stone that he cannot lift? This illustration from Max Shulman's story is actually heard occasionally from students. Dobie Gillis has easily identified its flaw. Except in clever stories, one might imagine that this fallacy would rarely occur. In fact, it occurs all the time in arguments such as we have seen above.

A principle contains within itself an internal inconsistency whenever it is framed in such a way that it undermines itself. One that is frequently heard on campus is this:

"All claims to truth are relative. There is no absolute truth."

If the claim of the principle itself ("all truth is relative") were true, then it would be false, for it is a claim to absolute truth. As we will see below in the discussion of relativism (pp. 109-13, 146-55 and 170-73), this notion is so common that it has achieved an almost worldview depth of commitment. At that level, it is unanalyzable; there is no effective argument against it.

Moreover, the general principle is given intellectual credibility by being framed in several ways by Friedrich Nietzsche and some well-known postmodern theorists. Consider these statements:

Nietzsche: Truth is "a mobile army of metaphors."[15]

If "truth is a mobile army of metaphors" is to mean anything substantial, it is itself a claim to literal truth. But there is no literal truth. So the statement is self-referentially incoherent.

Michel Foucault: "'Truth' is to be understood as a system of ordered procedures for the production, regulation, distribution, circulation, and operation of statements."[16]

This statement seems to say that "truth" is purely linguistic. But if that is so, then the sentence that says it is so is not about the nature of truth but only about the nature of language, and thus is self-referentially incoherent.

Richard Rorty: When we describe a giraffe, we need not try to describe it "as it really is. All we need to know is whether some competing description might be more useful for some of our purposes."[17]

This *pragmatic* view of truth means that truth is not found but constructed by language; whatever language gets you what you want is true. If Rorty's aim is to persuade philosophers to adopt this view of truth, he has not succeeded. Most philosophers disagree. When Rorty claimed that truth is whatever you can get your colleagues to believe, Alvin Plantinga remarked, "Richard, we are not going to let you get away with that." This, of course, turns the statement back upon itself, revealing, at least in this context, its uselessness.

Of course, Nietzsche, Foucault and Rorty have been well answered by their academic colleagues and critics. And even though none of the three seem to have recognized the fallacies inherent in their view, we do not need to be among them. Yet we do not need to reject all of their work. Even if the central theses of much of their work are flawed, each has contributed to the intellectual capital of current academic study. We can learn much from each of them about how language functions as power, as constructive of our understanding of reality, and of the tendency of words to replace concepts and concepts to replace reality.

But when the correct observation that different people have many different and contradictory views of reality becomes the philosophic principle that all of them are equally correct or valid, we must say no. (See chapters eight and eleven for ways to show that the recalcitrance of reality prevents us from practicing the philosophic principle of relativism.)

HYPOTHESIS CONTRARY TO FACT

In *hypothesis contrary to fact,* the contradiction at the heart of the fallacy is with reality itself. As Dobie Gilles says, "You can't start with a hypothesis that is not true and then draw any supportable conclusions from it." Still the attempt is made all the time, and in every area from politics to religion. Take politics for a moment:

> *"If Bush had not been elected, the United States would never have gone to war in Iraq."*
>
> *"If the United States had not dropped atomic bombs on Japan, the United States would have won World War II without causing nearly so many human casualties."*
>
> *"If Germany had not had a severe failure of intelligence, the Allies would have lost the war in Europe."*

It is easy to see that these often-expressed notions are only speculation. Maybe they would have been true, maybe not. But it's all *maybe.*

Now consider statements that Christians often hear.

> *"If you had not been brought up in a Christian home, you would never have become a Christian."*
>
> *"If we had copies of all the Lost Gospels, we would no longer trust the accounts in the New Testament."*
>
> *"If the apostle Paul had not been converted and become a spokesperson for the Christian faith, Christianity, if it had lasted till*

*today, would be utterly different. It was Paul who invented
Christianity."*

*"If the Crusades had not occurred, the Western world would not be
in major conflict with the Middle East."*

*"If we just learned not to take our religions so seriously, we would
get along much better with each other."*

Such sentiments can be multiplied almost without end. They have some
merit as possibilities, but none as serious contenders in religious arguments.
Without support in reality, they can never be considered as any more than
speculation.

Some of them assume as fact what may exist only in the imagination. We
have, for example, a few Gnostic Gospels deriving from the second century A.D.
They are no longer Lost Gospels. We know what they say; they have in fact en-
riched our understanding of the post-New Testament era, but they have not radically altered our understanding of the historical Jesus. Though this is contested
by a few scholars, the general consensus is that the texts are so colored by their
Gnostic origins that they are far less trustworthy than the four Gospels that have
been known from the beginning. In any case, it is sheer speculation to hold that
further "lost Gospels" will be found and that they will lead to a radically new understanding of Jesus. (See the bibliography on pp. 161-63.)

Christians too sometimes argue from premises contrary to fact. Consider
these:

*"If you would only read the Gospels, you would see that Jesus is the
Son of God and you would become a believer."*

*"If you had not been subjected to abuse as a child, you would be able
to see God as the great Father that he is."*

*"If you would just stop resisting the gospel, you would see that it is
true."*

"If you only read John Stott's **Basic Christianity,** *you would accept Christ as your Savior and Lord."*

Premises contrary to fact often express what we wish were true but isn't. We must learn to respond to reality as it is. We get nowhere dreaming about a past that can't be altered or a future that is not in our control. If, however, we turn some of our hypotheses contrary to fact into prayers, they are no longer merely dreams. Instead we are trusting God to bring about the reality that expresses his intentions for all of us—Christian and those we pray are on the way.

YOU HAVE INSULTED US ALL

Sentiment, False Analogy and Poisoning the Well

Polly Espy wept when she heard the tale of the man who needed a job to take care of his family. She thought it was a good idea to let students use their textbooks when they take tests. But she finally saw through the fallacy of calling one's opponent a liar. I should have done so well in the one time I encountered this fallacy. We will take each in turn.

SENTIMENT: *AD MISERICORDIAM*

Some of the truths of the Christian faith are hard to take. No one wants to be told that they or their friends are facing an after-life existence in hell. Surely a good God wouldn't send anyone to hell, would he? He loves us. I heard one pastor tell the congregation:

> *"I would never send anyone to hell. And God is surely kinder than I am."*

The problem is that Jesus would not have agreed. He warned of the awful punishment of hell several times (Mt 5:30; 25:30, 46; Mk 9:43-48; Lk 12:5). Here are three:

And if your right hand causes you to sin, cut it off and throw it away; it is better for you to lose one of your members than for your whole body to go into hell. (Mt 5:30)

But I will warn you whom to fear: fear him who, after he has killed, has authority to cast into hell. (Lk 12:5)

As for this worthless slave [a character in one of Jesus' parables], throw him into the outer darkness, where there will be weeping and gnashing of teeth. (Mt 25:30)

Of course, the most frequent argument denying the existence of hell is not the Scripture. It is the argument from sentiment. The punishment just seems too awful.

I must admit that I rarely bring up the topic of hell when I present a case for Christian faith. I, too, hate to face an audience with such bad news. Nor do I recommend that others stress the subject. This always seems to me too much like trying to scare people into heaven rather than drawing them there by emphasizing the love of God expressed in the agonizing sacrifice that Jesus made for us on the cross. Better to woo people to Christ through love, encouraging them to live for Christ as a citizen of the kingdom of God, than to frighten them into considering the Christian faith as a fire escape.

Still, I heard Francis Schaeffer say that if he had an hour to present the Christian gospel, he would spend the first forty-five minutes on judgment. Indeed, the truth of the existence of hell is part of the truth of the gospel, and it must not be denied or deliberately hidden from view.

When the objection to hell comes in the following form, I know that the objector has begun to understand the implications of the truth of the gospel. The comment often sounds like this:

"What about those who have never heard the gospel, who don't even know that Jesus ever existed? Surely God will not send them to hell. That would be unfair."

When a person makes this comment, I know that they have grasped the serious consequences of not accepting Christ as their own Lord and Savior. I also know that they may simply be raising the objection in order to avoid making a decision. Or, if they are especially hostile to the gospel, they may know that this question can turn the conversation away from the good news to what will appear such bad news that the Christian witness loses its credibility with others who are listening. In other words, the question may not be honest. How should a Christian answer?

I usually say something like this: "That's a very good question. Do you know what it means? It means that you understand how serious this issue is. But it also means that you have understood that Jesus offers salvation, and the answer to this particular question is now for you only academic. You have heard about Jesus. You will not be able to claim that you didn't know that commitment to him was the only way to eternal life."

I sometimes add, "And others here: you too have heard that Jesus is the only way to the Father. You will no longer have the excuse that you didn't know."

Then, in order to answer the serious objection that God is not fair (that is, not really good), I proceed to answer the question. How long my answer is will depend on how I assess the seriousness of the one who has objected and the character of others listening. My relatively full, nontechnical answer goes like this.

First, we must realize that God is really good. He made the universe to be a very good place, and he made human beings to live in it in harmony with both the world and himself. But we have rebelled against him, turned ourselves against God, against the world and against each other. This break in relationship would have continued forever and we would have created our own hell by virtue of our separation from him had not God himself stepped into our world, taken on the guilt of our rebellion and given us the opportunity to be returned to a good relationship with him. All we have to do is accept his sacrifice. Jesus the Son of God took our punishment on himself; he proclaimed on the cross that God had forsaken him. This was his hell for us. But he was resurrected and returned to fellowship with God.

It is because of his death and resurrection that when we die we can be with him for eternity.

"In my Father's house," Jesus said, "there are many dwelling places. If it were not so, would I have told you that I go to prepare a place for you?" (Jn 14:2). This comforting word is set in the immediate context of Jesus' own death and resurrection. Indeed, the apostle Peter assures us that God is not willing that any should perish but that all should come to repentance (2 Pet 3:9). The only way we find ourselves apart from God for eternity is if we reject him.

Now, I say to people, that means that those of us here know enough to follow this bit of truth toward a commitment of our lives to Christ. It also means that God will be fair to those who never hear this good news. I do not know specifically how he will handle this. Some say that everyone gets a chance to hear and accept Christ after death if they have not heard before. I don't find a scrap of evidence in Scripture for that. But I do find reason to believe that if persons recognize their separation from whatever they under-stand God to be and place their trust in God, their trust may be honored as saving faith. This is pictured by C. S. Lewis in his Narnia chronicle *The Last Battle*. The story is, of course, fiction and only a picture. But it may be one way that both God's justice and his love are worked out.

Then I remind people, for those of us here this is an academic answer. It has no other intellectual or spiritual import than to picture one way God is just and loving. By no means does it relieve any of us of our responsibility to choose. In fact, it will be impossible for us not to choose, for not to choose to follow Christ is to choose to reject him. As G. K. Chesterton said, "Hell is a monument to human dignity."

No one who finds himself or herself with a final destiny apart from God will be able to say to him, "That's not fair."

FALSE ANALOGY

I know of only a few objections to the Christian faith that fall precisely into the category of *false analogy*. Objections usually focus on ideas people don't like—such as sin, hell, the problem of suffering and evil, the authority or reliability of Scripture, the exclusivity of the Christian faith, the possibility of miracles, especially the resurrection of Jesus. But here is one false analogy:

> *"Religion is just a crutch. Stand on your own two feet. You don't need to rely on some deity to hold you up."*

As with many objections, as we have seen, there is a bit of truth to this one. We can accept the first part of the analogy. Christian faith is indeed a crutch. We need it because without Christ we fall on our face. We are broken people. The only question about Christianity as a crutch is whether it does the job. And it does.

Here is a second false analogy:

> *"Christians are like zombies. They don't think for themselves. They just follow their leaders and believe everything they say."*

This objection means that the objector has not met many genuine Christians. The objection is not only a false analogy but also *dicto simpliciter*, an unqualified generalization. The analogy might fit some groups that are generally considered cults, but hardly any of the people in the churches I know. Again, there *is* a grain of truth in the analogy. Some Christians are in fact anti-intellectual. It is often not that they do not think but that their thinking is limited to a particular theological perspective or narrow way of reading Scripture. Still within those hermeneutic systems, there is often a great deal of thoughtful and insightful Bible study. The best answer to the objection is to demonstrate your own ability to think well and to invite and take the objector to a church with a lively spiritual (and hopefully intellectual) life.

Other objections are similar to false analogy.

> *"The Bible is just a bunch of myths and fairy stories. It isn't a reliable guide to life any more than the stories of the Greek gods."*

A good, effective answer to this can be extensive. The likelihood is, however, that such an argument comes from someone who knows very little about the Bible. A short presentation of the various genres of the Bible's writings—law, history, poetry, proverbs, wedding song, drama (Job), Gospel (an utterly unique kind of biography unlike Greek or any other mythology), letters and apocalyptic narrative—can be helpful. One can also explain why, for example, the Gospels are likely to be fairly reliable accounts of Jesus' life.

Note: it is not necessary to argue for the divine inspiration of Scripture. That argument will not be very effective with those who have not yet become Christians. Nor does one have to argue for the inerrancy of Scripture—even if you hold this as important to mature Christian faith. You need to explain only the central character of Scripture, its account of God's dealing with humankind, especially as it involves Jesus. The goal of your answer is not so much to prove that Scripture is not mythology as to get seekers to read it, especially the Gospels. They will then forget about its looking like mythology. It doesn't.

POISONING THE WELL

Poisoning the well does not usually occur in conversations in the blatant form of calling your opponent a liar. That ploy is too obvious to be effective. Rather it occurs when the credibility of an authority the Christian spokesperson cites is summarily rejected. I am thinking of such examples as these:

> *"Phillip Johnson is a lawyer. How can he presume to challenge the theory of evolution?"*
>
> *"Theologians just don't get science."*
>
> *"He's not a scholar. He's a charismatic."*

When I was a student of English literature in graduate school, one of my colleagues once said,

"You're a fundamentalist, aren't you?"

Of course, in the educated world that's a severe slap in the brain pan. I had a good reply, though. I said, really without thinking about it, "No more than C. S. Lewis." To this my interlocutor said, "Oh." I had reestablished my intelligence.

Today in that same graduate school, that response might not work. Lewis is definitely "old school," good as a reference in medieval literature but probably not as someone to respect in religion or philosophy. A reference to J. R. R. Tolkien would work better—primarily, I think, because he was not so open with his serious Christian commitment.

One of my favorite examples occurred in a direct encounter with Richard Dawkins, author of *The Blind Watchmaker* and promoter of evolution by natural causes only. He had given a lecture on the nature of science, comparing his academic understanding with those of astrologers and the British tabloids. I was in the audience. In a formal question-and-answer session, I asked him why he did not compare his view of science to that of design scientist Michael Behe. Dawkins replied, "Well, Behe believes in God."

He paused for a moment to let that sink in. Then he added, "And besides that, Michael Behe is lazy."[1] He went on to say that the "irreducible complexities" Behe finds in the biosphere are not necessarily irreducibly complex. He should be looking for the explanation for how these complex structures could have been formed by natural "evolutionary pathways."

When I pointed out that this was *argumentum ad hominem* (argument against the man), Dawkins said, "Yes," but then went on to emphasize just how lazy Behe is.

Another man in the audience then said, "Professor Dawkins, I wonder if you know the problem we have here in the U.S. with people who want creation taught in the classroom." The specific question I asked never did get answered. Behe was, of course, not present. What can happen when the well that is poisoned is your own?

The most painful experience I ever had as a spokesperson for the faith involved a severe and very clever case of poisoning the well. It took place early one fall in the mid-1980s. I had been invited by the local InterVarsity group at Oberlin College to have a public dialogue with one of the school's philosophy professors. I knew from my hosts that he had grown up in a church and that, while he had become far more intellectual in character than was the church of his youth, he still maintained some links with the Christian faith. I met him before the dialogue, and we had a brief but friendly conversation.

In a dialogue or debate, I know that the one who makes the second presentation has an advantage. I always agree to go first, thinking that this will be the gracious thing to do. So to a packed room of perhaps two hundred students, I made the ten-to-fifteen-minute opening remarks. I told a story illustrating a simple basic principle that emphasizes the importance of one's understanding of the fundamental nature of reality. It was not intended as an argument for the existence of God, but as an argument for taking the question of God's existence as a serious matter. I intended to flesh out its implications in dialogue with the professor and the students.

Professor Jones (not his real name) got up and said incredulously:

"I don't know why you gave such an argument to these students. Everyone in this room knows what's wrong with it. You have insulted us all."

Then he went on to say, "If you want to present an argument for the existence of God, here is one that has some credibility." He then proceeded to present his own version of, as I recall, a cosmological argument. In my estimation, the argument had merit.

You can imagine my consternation as I waited for fifteen minutes as he presented his case. I was stunned. What could I say? How could I reply to such an *argumentum ad hominem*? Here's what was going on in my mind.

I didn't present an argument for the existence of God, did I? At this point, I wasn't sure. I know I did not intend to. I had never done so with that par-ticular story before. But I did not use notes. I didn't need them. Could I have, in the passion of the moment, turned an illustration into an argument?

I had previously been told by a colleague that a version of this story was to be found in the works of William James. *Is it possible that not only is this story there, but that the use to which I had put it had been refuted by James or someone after him?* I didn't know. Maybe Professor Jones had already assigned his students to analyze the story and refute it. After mulling this over as he presented his own case for the existence of God, I concluded that I didn't know enough to challenge Jones's charge that the story was fatally flawed and that the students knew this. Moreover, Jones was coming to the end of his presentation. It would soon be my turn to respond.

I thought I had two choices. First I could attempt to clarify what I had thought I had said and present the story again. But if there really was a fatal flaw in the story and Jones or one of students explained this flaw, I would be shown to be as dumb and inept as Jones said I was. Second, I could at-tempt to refute or show the weakness of Jones's own argument. But he was arguing for the existence of God. Why would I want to refute an argument for something I was hoping the students would themselves believe or come to believe? Reestablishing my own credibility was less important than that students believe in God. Third, I could thank Jones for his argument, make a few supporting comments and invite questions. This would leave my rep-utation in tatters, but it would honor God more than would a possibly failed attempt to regain a bit of my own dignity.

So I chose not to respond to Jones's personal attack. Rather I commended Jones for his argument and responded to the very few questions that ensued, knowing that I and my argument (or whatever it was) had been blown away.

I knew when I made my choice that I had lost all credibility in the minds of the nonbelieving Oberlin students. But I thought the InterVarsity chapter could fasten onto the now established authority of Professor Jones. I could not help them in their attempt to show the truth and relevance of the Chris-tian faith to the Oberlin campus. But Jones could.

This is not at all what happened. First, the Christian students were embarrassed by my performance. Their contender for the faith, their hero in the battle of campus ideologies, lay dead in the arena. As I walked across the campus to my guest room, no one walked with me. I had lost my credibility with them too. And I still had two more lectures to deliver to the chapter. You can imagine that they were sparsely attended and of little effect. The InterVarsity chapter itself went into a brown funk; its ministry to students languished for the remainder of that academic year. Three years passed before I was invited to speak there again.

Did I handle the situation as well as I could have done? Was there some other way than those I considered by which my credibility could have been recovered? That question plagued me for a very long time. First, I realized that I had not prepared adequately. I should have known if James or some other philosopher had used a story like mine and what happened when it was evaluated by subsequent philosophers.[2] Practice, practice, practice is fine, but it should be accompanied by prepare, prepare, prepare.

Second, I phoned a close friend, a philosopher who explores arguments in favor of Christian faith, and asked him what was wrong with the story and case that I presented. He assured me that I had done nothing wrong. "You were a victim of sophistry," he said. But he didn't help me to figure out what I should have done. Some years later he told me that he had met Jones and asked him about my encounter with him. He told me that Jones responded a bit awkwardly and said he had vowed not to do such dialogues again. Had Jones realized his own culpability? Did he regret being such a jerk? Hard to tell.

Third, it took several years, but eventually my emotional devastation subsided and I thought of another way I could have responded. On the one hand, after Jones's presentation and my commendation of his argument, I could have said, "Prof. Jones, could you tell me what you have understood my argument to be?" No matter what he responded, I could simply say,

"I'm amazed that you have interpreted my remarks this way.

Everyone in this room knows that's not what I intended. You have insulted all of us."

This would, of course, have leveled the field. But I would have responded to mud slinging by slinging mud myself. Moreover, if he was capable of using poisoning the well, he was probably capable of some other rhetorical skullduggery. The whole scene could have turned nasty.

I felt then and still feel that taking my lumps, letting myself be as a lamb led to the slaughter, was the better course to take. But I will allow others—you, dear readers—to disagree.

This was a terrible episode in my thirty or so years of speaking in defense of the Christian faith on campuses. But it is one from which I learned, and just as important to me if to no one else, nothing like it ever happened again.

FALLACIES AD INFINITUM

Still other fallacies in informal logic could be mentioned. In *non sequitur* the conclusion does not follow from the premises. Richard Dawkins's comment "Michael Behe believes in God" is a perfect example. There is no necessary connection between belief in God and bad science. The problem is that in today's secular universities such a connection is a reigning prejudice.

When the comment was made to Dawkins, "I wonder if you know the difficulty we have with people who want creation taught in the classroom," another type of fallacy was committed—the fallacy of the *red herring*. It is as if a stinking fish was dragged over the argument, reeking so much that attention was drawn away from the serious issue at hand, in this case: does science demand a foundation in metaphysical naturalism?

Polly Espy thought shouting was probably a fallacy. She was right. And so is bluster. And even humor when it becomes a red herring.

The eight fallacies that Shulman has illustrated in "Love Is a Fallacy," however, are the main ones. We will do well to learn what Polly did. After all, Christian apologists will gain more than a raccoon coat when their argument is persuasive because it is without logical flaw. Still, even a faultless argument may not convince. Happy thought? Yes. Only the Holy Spirit can assure what really counts—not just convincing but conviction.

PART TWO

GOOD ARGUMENTS
THAT OFTEN FAIL

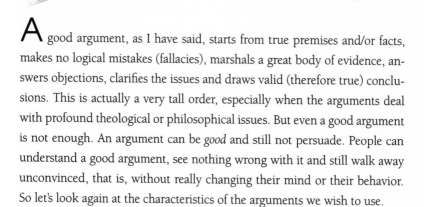

A good argument, as I have said, starts from true premises and/or facts, makes no logical mistakes (fallacies), marshals a great body of evidence, answers objections, clarifies the issues and draws valid (therefore true) conclusions. This is actually a very tall order, especially when the arguments deal with profound theological or philosophical issues. But even a good argument is not enough. An argument can be *good* and still not persuade. People can understand a good argument, see nothing wrong with it and still walk away unconvinced, that is, without really changing their mind or their behavior. So let's look again at the characteristics of the arguments we wish to use.

First, a good argument must start with true premises or accurate facts. This by itself is a tall order. If there is a disagreement on what the facts are or what the assumptions should be, there will be no progress. But let's say the parties agree.

Second, a good argument must be *valid;* that is, it must commit no logical errors either of the type discussed in part one or those associated with deductive reasoning in moving from its premises to its conclusion.[1]

Third, a good argument must be *sound;* that is, it must both be based on true premises and be valid. If an argument is sound, it will lead to true conclusions.

A good argument, however, needs one more characteristic to be what we would like it to be. It must be *convincing*. And this is the rub. What makes an argument convincing is often outside the control of the arguer. William Lane Craig reflects, for example, on the ineffectiveness of reasoning with people captivated by the assumptions of New Age or pantheistic thinking:

> *They assert that in Eastern thought the Absolute or the Real transcends the logical categories of human thought. They are apt to interpret the demand for logical consistency as a piece of Western imperialism. Trying to reason with such people can be very frustrating because they will cheerfully concede that their view is logically incoherent and yet insist that it is true.*[2]

As we shall see below, others who accept the norms of logical discourse will refuse to be convinced for reasons we simply cannot comprehend. The facts (or good arguments), so we Christians think, stare them in the face, and yet they do not see or comprehend or agree with the conclusions we so wish them to accept—that Jesus claimed to be God or that the resurrection happened or that an infinite and personal God exists.

Should we conclude, then, that our arguments are *ineffective*? Well, they didn't work, did they? Again Craig is helpful here. The person we're talking with is not likely, says Craig, "to just roll over and play dead the minute he hears your apologetic argument. Of course, he's going to disagree! Think of what's at stake for him."[3] We need study, practice and patience in our witness. Craig adds that "being 'convincing' is person-relative. Some people will simply refuse to be convinced."[4] His final counsel is worth quoting in full:

> *What we need to develop is an apologetic that is both cogent [what I have called sound] and persuasive to as many people as possible. But we must not be discouraged and think our apologetic is ineffective if many or even most people find our arguments unconvincing. Success in witnessing is simply communicating Christ in the power of the Holy Spirit and leaving the results*

to God. Similarly, effectiveness in apologetics is presenting cogent and per-
suasive arguments for the Gospel in the power of the Holy Spirit, and leav-
ing the results to God.

Of course, some of our presentations are just not very good. Some contain precisely the sorts of logical fallacies we have just examined. They *should* not persuade.

But there is irony here. When people are open to the gospel, eager to hear how it addresses their despair and offers hope, they come to believe in spite of the meagerness of our efforts. The Holy Spirit overcomes our ineptness and uses our rather paltry attempts anyway. This does not excuse us, but it does put us in our place!

Still, let us assume our arguments are good, yet they often fail to persuade. There are a host of reasonable explanations for these failures. Here is a taxonomy of those explanations:

1. Failures of the one who defends Christian faith
   - arrogance, aggression and cleverness
   - misreading the audience
   - misjudging their ability to reason
   - misjudging their existential interests
2. Failures of the cultural background: the worldview factor
   - the issue of evolution
   - the issue of relativism
3. Failures of the audience
   - moral refusal

Throughout part two I will continue to interlace illustrations of my own failures and successes—more the former than the latter. I think I have learned far more from failures than successes; I certainly remember them better.

5

PEOPLE CAN'T COMMUNICATE. WHAT?

Arrogance, Aggression and Cleverness

In presentations of the case for Christ, good rational arguments often do not persuade. I mean by "a good argument" one that starts from true premises and/or facts, makes no logical mistakes (fallacies), marshals a great body of evidence, answers objections, clarifies the issues and draws valid (therefore true) conclusions.

Here is the experience of one young would-be defender of the faith who later became a professor of philosophy. George Mavrodes was invited to the house of a fellow Christian to have conversation with a young man who proclaimed himself an atheist.

> I was eager to make a rational conversation, so I unloaded on the poor unbeliever an argument that I thought was really strong: a version of C. S. Lewis's moral argument for the existence of God. I was stunned when I saw that the argument was apparently having no bite at all. When the evening ended, the friend was, so far as I know, no closer to theism than he was when we first met.[1]

Mavrodes's experience is typical. When such rational arguments are made in the field of Christianity, they are often not just ignored but rejected. Why is this?

Aristotle overstated the case, but still we should heed the warning it contains:

Every failure of Truth to persuade reflects the weakness of its advocates.

This is a humbling reminder of our responsibility as Christians: we must make the best presentation of the gospel that we can make. Of course, we are limited in our ability—every one of us, the clever and the not so bright. Our Lord knows this and works around our limitations. But we are responsible to do our best.

In short, we should not only learn the best arguments for the faith; we should also learn how to present these in the most persuasive way. Reason alone is not enough. It must combine with rhetoric.[2] As we focus on arrogance, aggression and cleverness, we will begin to see some of what this means. We start with the principle.

THE PRINCIPLE

> **Valid, well substantiated arguments presented with arrogance, aggression or an overly clever attitude are often not heard clearly enough to attract the attention they deserve.**

Arguments can be presented with passion and commitment without projecting arrogance. Arrogance on the part of the one who speaks for Christ sends the wrong message. The argument is more likely to be rejected than accepted.

In the late 1960s, a well-known Christian apologist, who often gave public speeches defending the faith, debated a well-known God-is-dead theologian. The apologist was urged by a pastor friend to "destroy" the heretical theologian—that is, to make his foolishness so obvious that the theologian would never again get a job at a university.

The Christian speaker went on the attack, ridiculing the theologian in the tone and tenor of his remarks as well as the logical substance. The effect was precisely the opposite of what was intended. Though many agreed that the apologist had won the debate, they were so offended by his aggression, insults and arrogance that they were utterly unmoved to agree with him. The traditional Christians were divided: some lauded the apologist as their champion, but most, including the sponsors of the debate, recognized that he had convinced only the already convinced. No one on the fence or on the other side appeared to change their mind. They could not get past the offensive arrogance and meanness of the apologist.

I don't think he ever lectured for that organization again. Unfortunately, there are still public apologists who continue to use this approach. And there are too many Christians who take glee in sponsoring them.

InterVarsity staff member Gary Deddo says that once when a noted apologist was presenting his case for Christianity, an international student asked a question about a technical point. The apologist replied curtly, "You just haven't read the literature." Of course he hadn't read the literature! What was the literature? He had no way to know.

In a book aptly titled *Humble Apologetics,* John Stackhouse recalls hearing a sophisticated, well-argued university lecture by an overly self-confident apologist. Stackhouse recalls that, as a young Christian who loved apologetics, he was delighted. Then he overheard a student tell her friend, "I don't care if the son of a bitch *is* right, I still hate his guts."[3] She had, it appears, observed the apologist engage in what Stackhouse calls "intellectual browbeating."[4]

Some apologists can be clever. What is it about Ravi Zacharias that allows him to be clever and intellectually sharp without offending? Deddo believes it's the "existential" quality of his presence. Zacharias shows that he feels deeply for the situation of people today, not just for his own approach to elucidating the gospel. It takes an apologist with special gifts to pull off clever humor directed in any way toward a person asking a question in public. Apologists must preserve the dignity of the person asking even the most silly or perverse of questions.[5]

My own approach to witness is, I trust, considerably more gentle. I try hard to be fair to those who disagree and to treat them kindly, realizing that I will probably learn a great deal from them. Although earlier in my ministry I participated in debates, I soon learned to reject the word *debate* in public promotions. I now tell my hosts that I will be pleased to *dialogue* with a professor or a pundit, but I will not approach my role as a typical debater. I will not go for the jugular. Rather, I "go for a draw." I am pleased if, in the process of the public dialogue, a good portion of the central truths of the Christian faith are given a hearing in the light of the opposing views of other partners in the dialogue.

I am interested in seeing Christians understand the alternatives and non-Christians recognize the strength of the Christian view. Whenever this has been the ethos of the public sessions, I have never had a bad experience. I have dialogued with atheist philosophers, New Agers and proponents of Eastern religions, sometimes one on one, sometimes on a panel with several. I believe the gospel has been heard in these encounters and no one has been offended.

I have, however, had two especially negative experiences. One, at Oberlin College, I recounted in the previous chapter. The other took place at Bowling Green University in Ohio. I had been asked by an organization to debate a local philosophy professor. My response was to insist that it not be billed as a "debate," and I thought that would be the case. Instead, when I arrived, the campus was plastered with posters announcing "The Great Debate." A second Christian student group that likes to sponsor "debates" had joined in the promotion, and the word *debate* became prominent in the advertising.

Troubled by this, I met with the professor for coffee. We got along well, and I relaxed some. The debate attracted so many students that not only was the large lecture room filled but students spilled over into two other rooms where they watched on TV screens.

The debate proceeded. We both made presentations, responded to each other and invited questions. The tone of our remarks was respectful of each other, with the exception of one low blow by my opponent who likened the

Gospels to Republican political speeches touting their candidate. I thought that this remark was a bit nasty but so obviously over the top that it didn't need a response. As the evening ended, I felt satisfied that at least some good had been done.

While I relaxed with friends afterward, thinking all had gone reasonably well, I learned that the Christian sponsors—leaders in both organizations—were quite displeased. I saw myself as saving a "debate" by turning it into a "dialogue." They saw me as "losing the debate." I could not convince them that what they were looking for was in the long run counterproductive. You see, even though I made a good case for my approach, I lost that argument too. Maybe I should have turned aggressive and at least made that debate entertaining.

Perhaps Bill Watterson puts his cartoon pen on our common human nature—both Christian and otherwise—when he has Calvin tell Hobbes that people seem just to "shout at each other nowadays. I think it's because conflict is drama. Drama is entertaining, and entertainment is marketable." Civil discourse is not; it's too dull, no fireworks. When Hobbes says, "Hmm, you may be right," Calvin replies, "What a boring day this turned out to be."[6]

To my experience at Bowling Green, however, there was a "page two: the rest of the story," as Paul Harvey would say. A few weeks after the Great Debate, I received a letter from the philosophy professor. He wrote,

> This is a belated thanks for *The Universe Next Door*. Now that the semester has come to an end I've had a chance to examine it. Although no one could read the book without observing that you have a definite point of view, your treatment of the several non-Christian worldviews is both lucid and fair. I wouldn't hesitate to give it to my students.
>
> Let me say again that I enjoyed our exchange in Bowling Green. You were an unapologetic apologist, polished and professional but also someone who connects well with an audience of undergraduates (and others). I wouldn't at all mind if fate leads us sometime again to share

a podium. And it would be a considerable pleasure to down another half-dozen cups of coffee while chatting with you.

Suffice it to say, this letter put a spring in my step that had been lacking. In fact, the whole incident has heightened my desire to convince Christians that the Christian faith is best promoted when the Christian character of Christianity is demonstrated in the very rhetorical style of its presentation. True Christian faith respects other people even when you think they are wrong. So should its apologetics.[7]

Francis A. Schaeffer had an experience much like mine. He debated controversial Episcopal Bishop James Albert Pike in Chicago in the late 1960s. They both treated each other well, and no sparks flew. Conservative Christians were disappointed. But Schaeffer had by his demeanor won the heart of Pike, who soon after invited Schaeffer to his home. There Schaeffer was able to counsel him about his son who had just committed suicide.

Cleverness too can have the same effect as arrogance; in fact, it may be arrogance without much of a disguise. Many years ago at a junior college near my home, College of DuPage, I gave a lecture on Christianity and Eastern mysticism. During the presentation, I was interrupted by a student who said, "But people can't communicate."

Neither today nor then do I remember why he made this objection. I can't think of anything that prompted it. Anyway, he said it and I replied. I cupped my hand in back of my ear and said, "What?"

"People can't communicate," he repeated.

"What?" I responded, leaning closer.

"People can't communicate," he said again.

"What?" I said, and he quickly got up and walked out of the room.

I lost him as a fellow dialoguer. I had caught the student in self-referential incoherence. If people can't communicate, it makes no sense to try—but he tried anyway.

I lost the audience as well. The atmosphere in the room became tense. I had the power position; the student was at my mercy, and I was merciless.

There would have been many ways I could have probed what the student said and gently let him off the hook so that both the he and the audience could see the issue clearly. Instead they rightfully took offense at my cleverness.

I have vowed never to do that again. And I have largely kept my vow. Only once since then did I apparently treat a questioner too harshly. I was pointing out the internal inconsistency of a student's "relativism," and while at the time I did not think I had put too much pressure on the student, I learned later that at least the Christian part of the audience thought I had gone too far. Had I done so? Perhaps. But just as likely, the Christian students' own faith was more imbued with relativism than it should have been. Perhaps they felt targeted too.

There is an opposite rhetorical error that some Christians can make—that is to be so distant and unfeeling that neither passion nor compassion comes through.[8] I once heard a Christian philosopher make a formal presentation of a particular answer to the question of whether those who have not heard the gospel are lost. Reflecting on this, one of my Christian friends said, "If that's Christianity, I don't want it." Though I did not have the same response as my friend, I was not convinced that the philosopher was correct. Did my intellectual response stem from his cold presentation, or did I think his argument was weak for other reasons? I don't know. It's sometimes hard to sort out just why an argument is or is not effective. The principle is clear, though: Good reason and apt rhetoric belong together. Unless it's sushi or smoked salmon, raw fish is not very tasty.

Note this well: "Good relationships with people" (love) is not more important than truth. Rather, the propagation of truth requires good relationships with people.

Remember the final phrases of the apostle Peter's definition of apologetics: "Do this [defend the faith] with gentleness and respect, keeping a clear conscience, so that those who speak maliciously against your good behavior in Christ may be ashamed of their slander" (1 Pet 3:15-16 NIV). It really is better to "lose" an argument and gain a friend. You can have many more dialogues with the friend.

I DON'T GET IT

Misreading the Audience

Arrogance, aggression and cleverness are major barriers to persuasion. But so is misreading the audience. Except for coercive persuasion, which some groups use to force their views on others, the audience controls the outcome of every argument. That two plus two is four may be obvious to you and the rest of the adult world, but not to a young child learning arithmetic for the first time. So too, a clear presentation of the case for the resurrection of Jesus may convince many people that Jesus did in fact rise from the dead, but it does not convince everyone.

Here we will examine several reasons for this—the necessarily abstract and/or complex nature of some arguments, lack of existential interest in the issue at stake, the varying limitations of human intelligence and the occasional presence of psychological barriers.

THE ABSTRACT FACTOR

> **Many excellent arguments, especially in classical apologetics, are so highly abstract that they make little or no personal impact even on those who do not disagree with their conclusions.**

The premises may be true and accepted as true, the argument may be valid and seen to be valid, the conclusion may therefore be true, but the argument itself does not *convince.* The person you would like to move closer to the truth just says, "Okay. I understand. The argument looks correct. But so what?"

Over the years, I have thought about the classical arguments for the existence of God. Some of them, such as those of René Descartes, I have studied. Like many who have analyzed Descartes's arguments, I think they fail for a variety of reasons. So they make no impact on me because, while I believe it is true that God exists, I don't think Descartes's arguments actually prove this. They do nothing to shore up my faith. I believe in God's existence for other and, for me, much more telling reasons.[1]

But there are other arguments than those of Descartes. One is the kalam argument, an ancient argument that modern Christian apologists have resurrected and refined. Fashioned first by Arabic philosophers in the Middle Ages, this cosmological argument moves from the notion that the universe must have had a beginning to the notion that this beginning must have been caused to the conclusion that this cause must be personal. The argument is highly sophisticated, and it takes Christian philosopher J. P. Moreland twenty-four pages to present and defend it.[2] Finally, he concludes:

> *In summary, it is most reasonable to believe that the universe had a beginning which was caused by a timeless, immutable agent. This is not a proof that such a being is the God of the Bible, but it is a strong statement that the world had its beginning by the act of a person. And this is at the very least a good reason to believe in some form of theism.*[3]

The specific argument and its details are not important here. What is important is the kind of conclusion that is drawn: There is "a good reason to believe in some form of theism." The problem is that to believe in "some form of theism" is not very attractive, not very existentially satisfying. The conclusion—a personal creator must exist—is a long way from showing that the biblical God exists and that Jesus is Savior and Lord; in fact this goal, toward which a defense of Christian faith must tend, is not even on the distant horizon. The argument leads only to a certain philosophic system, not to a robustly holy God who has created us, holds us accountable for how we behave and rescues us even when we fail. A full-fledged Christian theism is, of course, "some kind of theism," but the latter is not itself enough to set one's heart on fire, not enough to draw many people to Christ as Lord and Savior.[4]

Still, for those who are convinced by the kalam argument that some sort of God exists, the door is now open to consider just what kind of God this might be. Abstract arguments certainly have a role to play.

Douglas Geivett outlines an argument with many steps, beginning with the kalam argument and ending with belief in Jesus.[5] But, so it seems to me, every step in the argument can be (and has been) challenged, and every step is important. Probability (which almost always is all one can ask for each step) decreases each time it must be invoked. That makes the entire argument, I should think, rather improbable—not false, be advised, but solely as an argument not very probable either.

Parallel arguments do not suffer from this weakness. If one can give a half-dozen independent probable arguments for the same notion, the probability increases. This is what Richard Swinburne does in a philosophically sophisticated way in *The Existence of God.*[6] Still, his argument is the epitome of abstraction and can appeal only to the intellect of the intellectual—not a bad thing to do, of course, but it is a limited audience.

There is an alternative to such abstract arguments that I believe is more useful in addressing most people, including those who are quite well educated. It is predicated on the notion that the best reason for believing in Jesus is Jesus himself. So I suggest that one who seeks to defend the faith begin with the biblical testimony about Jesus. When objections arise—"Why should I believe the Bible?" for example—they can be addressed or shunted to the side for the moment. The point is to get people to "look at" and, in a deeper sense, to "meet" Jesus in the Gospels. He is a compelling figure. The word about him does not come back void. Conviction comes from an encounter with Jesus as prompted by the Holy Spirit. Abstract arguments become academic when a person meets Jesus.

Of course, most mature apologists who are interested in such abstract arguments know that this is the case. They realize that their arguments will appeal only to those especially gifted to understand complex reasoning. Those who are just learning the craft, however, may easily acquire skill in abstract argument and mistake that for skill in the whole art of defending the faith. Abstract arguments have a value in assuring thoughtful Christians that their faith has some rational justification. After all, as longtime Inter-Varsity staff member Tom Trevethan says, "The heart will not long rejoice in what the mind knows is not true." Christians should begin to understand some of these arguments, if not for their immediate witness to nonbelievers, then for their own confidence that when such arguments are helpful, as with those who are philosophically minded, they are there to be used. But their use is limited. If people feel that all our arguments for the faith are just so many abstract arguments, we will not likely be effective witnesses to our life-giving Lord.

Again, Christians do not waste their time when they investigate these arguments. To those with philosophic interest and ability, they can be valuable in showing that the biblical notion of God has features that can be shown to be reasonable. It is not irrational to believe that a Being with these features exists. In fact, it may be the most rational belief of all.

The mistake is for Christians to believe that once they have mastered the kalam argument and other abstract philosophic proofs and are able to present them clearly and accurately, these arguments will attract attention to the gospel or convince anyone of even the minimal content they claim to prove. Having these arguments may trigger a confidence in one's arguments that is undeserved and misleading.[7] Even those non-Christians who can and do follow these abstract arguments can easily say, "Okay. So what?" And it's hard to answer that question without shifting ground to a less abstract approach which might better have been taken from the start.

John Wilson, editor of the Christian intellectual journal *Books and Cul-*

ture, himself a Christian who understands complex abstracts, has this to say:

> I don't despise the traditional proofs for the existence of God, as some con-
> temporary philosophers do, but neither do they compel assent. This is no
> doubt my own fault; I am allergic to the sort of thought from which such
> proofs are constructed, just as—by and large—I am allergic to symphonies
> (chamber music is another thing completely). But there are also "peculiar"
> proofs for God's existence such as those proposed by Carlos Eire.[8]

Here he cites Eire's proof from "desire."[9] My point is not to abandon the
use of abstract arguments, only to understand their limitations and the fact
that they do not convince even those well capable of understanding them.[10]

LACK OF INFORMATION

> **Sometimes simple lack of information stands in the way of the
> effectiveness of a rational argument.**

Every argument assumes some facts that are not in immediate evidence.
Every witness has to start somewhere, and we Christians have a tendency to
assume that people have information they simply do not have. It is very easy
to do.

As I write this, Mel Gibson's *The Passion of the Christ* has just been released. One of my friends. who was raised in one of the stricter Protestant
denominations, came away from the movie very angry. She said, "I went to
the movie to learn about Jesus, but I didn't learn anything."

I took her to mean that she had a solid idea of who Jesus was and nothing
had been added to her storehouse of detail. So I defended the movie by
pointing out several direct quotations from the Gospels that had deep theological import. She did not contest this but insisted that the movie was too
superficial theologically. I later learned that what had angered her was that

she had been able to see only the graphic nature of Jesus' suffering. She did not recognize the profound theological symbolism of many of the graphic details; nor did she understand the radical nature of statements like "I am the way, and the truth, and the life. No one comes to the Father except through me" (Jn 14:6). Nor did she grasp the significance of Jesus' struggle in the Garden of Gethsemane. I am not even sure she understood that Jesus himself believed that he was taking on the sins of all humankind as he died, though she may have understood something of the concept in the abstract.

My response to her anger was, as near as I can now tell, utterly off the point. I could have helped her with the background theology. Then my comments about the effectiveness of the film and its use of graphic violence might have carried some weight.

As witnesses we need to know as much as we can about what those we speak with know. If they have little or no church experience, they may not be ready even to begin to understand our arguments, let alone agree with them. The arguments will be irrelevant.

Let's take a second illustration. Say you have asked a person, "Do you believe in God?" "Yes," they respond. Now ask. "Who or what do you think God is?" The answers will vary widely. Some will give an answer from within a traditional Christian faith—God as triune. Many, however, will say God is a force—something to get the universe going, but not personally engaged with human affairs.[11] Some will see God as the impersonal divine substratum of all reality, the fire that fuels the universe, and each of us as a spark of this divine fire. You and I and all people are really divine, gods looking for unity with the One impersonal God.

This is something like what Shirley MacLaine must have meant when, in the TV version of *Out on a Limb,* she ran up and down the ocean beach waving her hands and saying, "I am god. I am god." A lot of confusion will have to be cleared up before a case for Christian faith can even begin to be made.

Others will see God as Allah, a personal God who is solely one, not triune. Still others will say they believe in God as a necessary projection of our human longing for a cosmic Father who will ease our anxieties and give us meaning. The list of concepts is a mile long. Here in their own words, for example, are several more views garnered from students at Michigan State University, Bryn Mawr College and Haverford College:[12]

> *"A beautiful person w/only kindness in mind. The person does not even know the definition of evil."*
>
> *"I get a feeling rather than a really concrete picture of what he's really like. . . . I think of warmth & colors & brightness—he makes me smile. He listens to me. He talks to me in his way. . . . He has a great & wonderful love that I find difficult to describe . . . only that it is always present . . . & I can feel it. I think of him as caring & loving. The feeling I get when I think of him is indescribable. . . . It's everything good & wonderful all rolled up in one."*
>
> *"God is someone, a female of course, who loves everything it [sic] has created and is very protective of what she has created."*
>
> *"I believe in divinity, in fact I believe that there are many gods. . . . The gods are those who created the universes [sic], and maintain balance and order. I follow/worship the gods because I seek to know them and be in balance with them and my world."*

We'll stop here. The point is that when we talk about God, people may not be able to understand what we are saying; we may think we are on the same page but not even be in the same book.

Jesus Christ as the New Testament presents him is also an obscure figure to many. Even if a person says they believe that he is the Son of God, this may mean very, very little to them. Just what they actually understand would come to the surface if we asked them, "What do you mean when you say Jesus is the Son of God?" Much defense of the faith must necessarily involve a great deal of fairly ordinary revelation of information, one might even say proclamation. We just need to witness to who and what God and Jesus (and a host of other ideas and issues) are.

John Stackhouse recounts an airline conversation. His seatmate had just told him she was a graduate of the University of Chicago, on her way to take a manager's job in a Napa Valley winery. He told her he taught world religions at a secular university and then bemoaned that many of his students could not place Jesus and the apostle Paul in the "correct chronological order." "Who is this 'Apostle Paul' you are referring to?" she asked.[13]

When we present a case for Christian faith, we had best do so with as much knowledge of our audience's knowledge as we can ferret out without being obnoxiously nosey. When we are speaking with our friends, we are on the firmest ground, for then the argument can proceed slowly enough to be wisely framed.

THE EPISTEMIC EQUIPMENT FACTOR

> **All but a few human beings are capable of rational thought, but they are not equally endowed. In technical terms, everyone's epistemic equipment is not equally powerful.**

There are those with big minds, small minds and every size of mind in between. Some people simply can't understand some arguments, especially complex abstract arguments. Others not only can understand them but can and do give apologists fits when they use them.

Let us return to the kalam argument. This argument has been subjected to a variety of criticisms, and these have, in turn, been answered by those who find it convincing. Even at the lowest level, the argument is accessible only to those who are able to think at a high level of abstraction. Not all can do so.

There is, after all, a deep mystery to the experience of seeing something to be true. Indeed, there is a deep mystery to consciousness itself, and it is in consciousness that the experience of seeing something to be true resides. Consider unexpectedly meeting your brother on a street in a foreign city. How do you recognize him? There are a host of reasons. But how did you do it? He appeared. You saw. You knew. You are using your epistemic equipment, of course, but how did it work? And why did you draw the correct conclusion? I think it is fair to say, no one knows.

Now change the situation. You are looking at a short column of figures and trying to add them. Two plus two: what's the answer? You don't think about it, you know as soon as you see the numbers. But what about a long column of figures in the hundreds? You go through the mental operations you learned years ago and conclude that the sum is 10,262. How did you do it? Why were you sure? Well, you aren't. So you add them several times, getting the same answer. You may now be more psychologically certain, but you may still be wrong. You could have made the same "stupid" mistake each time you added. So you add them on a calculator. You still get the same number. But did you misenter a number (one of a number of possible "stupid" mistakes), so that you got the same wrong answer as when you added them "by hand"? You can be psychologically certain because you have repeated a process on which you rely, but you can still be wrong.

Now make the exercise more complex. You know basic arithmetic; you have grasped algebra and analytical geometry. You know what you are trying to accomplish when you work a problem in calculus. But try as you will, you cannot see why any particular answer is correct. You just don't get it. So you get help from a tutor but still don't get it. You have reached the end of your ability to increase your knowledge of mathematics, at least for now. If you are like I was in my first calculus course, you get help from your fiancée, who is a mathematical whiz, but you still don't get it. Then, because you do have some mental acumen, you drop the course before you have to receive a grade. I have not tried to understand calculus for over fifty years. Could I have "gotten it" and gone forward? I don't know. Could I "get it" now? I don't know. I only know that so far I haven't done so.

This is the mind's experience of every type of argument—mathematical, philosophical, theological, historical. Either you see how the argument proceeds and "see" whether it is valid, or you never catch on to what's at stake in the argument. "Words, words, words," Hamlet said. Yes, words and numbers, but no significance. "A tale told by an idiot, full of sound and fury, signifying nothing": such are many of the arguments we hear for all kinds of views—political, religious, psychological.

The point is that some of the arguments we use as Christians simply mean nothing to those we are addressing. I believe that this is the case with arguments for all sorts of ideas we would like people to believe. Seeing, understanding, grasping the truth of an argument—all of these are private matters, matters of the conscious mind; and on this issue the mind is impenetrable. Either we see or we don't.

Jesus recognized this, and more than once he appeared nonplussed. Philip had asked Jesus to show him the Father. "Don't you know me, Philip," Jesus replied, "even after I have been among you such a long time?" Then he gave Philip a "reason" for his frustration: "Anyone who has seen me has seen the Father. How can you say, 'Show us the Father'? Don't you believe that I am in the Father, and that the Father is in me?" (Jn 14:9-10 NIV).

When Jesus realized that Philip had not understood who Jesus was by directly living with Jesus, he took another approach. Jesus gave him a principle to use: If you have seen me, you have seen the Father. Philip had seen Jesus. The conclusion was obvious. Did the argument work? We don't know. We don't have Philip's response, though the text seems to imply he did. Certainly we as readers are supposed to "see."

I will conclude this chapter with a factor that does not fit easily into any of the above categories. It is a *nonrational* reason, or perhaps better to say *cause,* for the failure of some quite rational arguments.

PSYCHOLOGICAL BLOCKS

> **Some people who do not profess the Christian faith are especially resistant to some of its key ideas because of events in their lives that have personally scarred them. Rational arguments therefore miss the mark.**

Three situations illustrate this principle. First, some people in their child-hood or youth have been molested by a parent. Or their father has been a tyrant to them. Escaping him by growing up has been a great relief. Their notion of their earthly father is inevitably linked to their notion of God as Father. As a result, the notion of the fatherhood of God becomes a barrier to Christian belief. Why would they seek out a cosmic Being like their own father but stronger and even more demanding?

Rational argument is likely to have little positive effect. What is needed is psychological healing, and that is more likely to come not through rational arguments but through experiencing genuine love from within a community of Christians. Such a person needs to see at least a few good earthly fathers. For them the observation of a father's or a mother's love for their own and others' children may work wonders. If love from a Christian community is added to that, the barrier may be breached. Love is not just the final apolo-getic, as Francis A. Schaeffer said, but the first as well.

As a person grows in psychological and emotional health, he or she can also begin to experience intellectual growth. A theology of "Our Father who art in heaven" may then appear not only true to them but attractive. Jesus' own love for his Father, expressed so profoundly in the Upper Room dis-course of John 13–17, may then come to life for them: "Do not let your hearts be troubled. Believe in God, believe also in me. In my Father's house there are many dwelling places. If it were not so, would I have told you that I go to prepare a place for you? And if I go and prepare a place for you, I will come again and will take you to myself, so that where I am, there you may be also" (Jn 14:1-4).

Sharing the gospel with such people means sharing much more than in-formation; it means sharing one's life.[14]

A second situation likewise can become a psychological block. Psycho-logical reticence often develops after a child or a youth has bad experience(s) in a church community. Some churches are extremely demanding with re-gard to lifestyle. "Thou shalt not do anything that is fun, hip, cool, rad, what all the kids are doing—in other words, worldly." In former times Catholic schools had more than their share of nuns who ruled with a ruler. And Protestant churches have often majored in a long list of don'ts.

At the other extreme are children and youth who experience no restraints at all from either their parents or the church. Anything goes. So as adults they look back on their church as wimpish, silly, unrealistic about what should be taught and modeled about character development. A Christianity that does not provide guidance to children and youth is not worth considering when you grow up.

Any case for Christian faith for these people must include a good deal of clarifying of *what* Christian faith is. To launch into an argument regarding its truth may well be premature.

Finally, in a third illustration, consider the psychological damage done by tightly controlled religious cults. In such groups ordinary members are required to accept a list of beliefs—many of them not just dubious but downright false. They must not only accept them without question but promote them in intense and aggressive evangelistic outreach. To leave the group is to lose one's salvation. Sometimes a cult member realizes that what they have been taught is not true and that they have been manipulated by the leaders. Once they have succeeded in coming out of the group, they have no intention of getting involved in any other group that proclaims an exclusive message.

Hard, practical love is again both the first and final apologetic for someone with this background. For a while it may be the only apologetic.

ARGUMENTS THAT WORK

The aim of every Christian witness should be to construct arguments that really work. In part three I will suggest some that have done that. For now, note that learning to read the audience, learning to understand those to whom you are witnessing, is vital. Listen carefully to what they say, ask lots of questions, don't jump in with irrelevant comments or statements that are not sensitive to what you are learning about them. These are not easy tasks, and they will not guarantee success, but they will make it far more likely.

WHAT A HAREBRAINED IDEA!

Worldviews and Evolution

The most significant rational reason that keeps arguments from being persuasive is the gap that often exists between the worldview of the presenter and that of the audience. Arguments rest on background assumptions—ideas that are taken so much for granted that they don't have to be articulated. When Richard Dawkins said, "Michael Behe believes in God" (see p. 63 above), he was not just making a statement about Behe's religious commitment. He was relying on the other scientists in the audience to believe that no one who believes in God could be a good scientist. He did not have to argue for this. It is just such worldview commitments that block naturalists from giving theistic arguments any consideration at all.[1]

Take this simple case. Joe, let us say, has been dying of rapidly spreading cancer. Everyone—his Christian family, the doctors, Joe himself—is certain he will soon die. Then without any particular medical reason, Joe suddenly begins to improve. In a few days, he is up and running and back at work. The doctors say they can find no trace of the "deadly" cancer. It's a miracle, say Joe and his family. Two of his doctors, however, are less quick to agree. Things like this happen, they say. We don't know why, but you can never be sure about a disease, even one as deadly as the cancer Joe suffered from. A third doctor is quite certain that there has been no miracle. Miracles can't happen, he says. There is no God, no spiritual forces, nothing outside the ordinary working of matter in space and time. Whatever happened was natural.

Most Christians rarely use the category of miracle to explain extraordinary events. Even the so-called miracles performed by the saints are subjected to long study and analysis before they are declared miracles by the Catholic Church. But Christians do believe miracles can happen. There is really nothing outlandish in thinking that some events in our world are brought about by God in his providential care for the world. God made the world; he is utterly in charge of everything that occurs. Miracles are more amazing for their infrequency than for their occurrence, but nothing is impossible with God.

Naturalists, however, are like Richard Dawkins (who claims to be a "fulfilled atheist") or Carl Sagan (who believes that "the cosmos is all there is, all there was and all there ever will be"). No amount of evidence will convince them of a miracle. A natural explanation can be imagined—if not proved—for every event that might occur. If there is nothing outside the natural world, then there is no need to locate the precise reasons for the occurrence of an unusual event. The cause was natural. It had to be.

This illustration is only one example of a much more general principle.

THE WORLDVIEW PRINCIPLE

> **A person's worldview limits the views that can be consistently held. No argument whose conclusion is obviously inconsistent with one's worldview can be rationally convincing unless the worldview itself is adjusted.**

This principle may seem obscure at first, but its meaning becomes clear with a little explanation. First, we need to understand the notion of *worldview.*

A worldview is a fundamental commitment to a way of understanding the world. In common parlance, a worldview is a philosophy of life. Everyone has one. Here is a formal definition.

*A worldview is a commitment, a fundamental orientation of the heart, that
can be expressed as a story or in a set of presuppositions (assumptions which
may be true, partially true or entirely false) which we hold (consciously or
subconsciously, consistently or inconsistently) about the basic constitution of
reality and that provides the foundation on which we live and move and
have our being.*[2]

This definition needs to be unpacked. We will start with its pretheoretical
character.

A MATTER OF THE HEART

Worldviews are rooted deep in the *heart*. They are fundamental commitments. They seem so true that one cannot imagine them being otherwise. Alfred Whitehead says that "some assumptions appear so obvious that people
do not know what they are assuming because no other way of putting things
has ever occurred to them."[3] These assumptions reside in the background of
all our thinking. They are controlling beliefs that make it difficult, if not impossible, for a person to consider as true anything that they know contradicts these commitments.

Philosopher William J. Wainwright says that people who reject religious
ideas don't usually do so for specific, well-formulated intellectual reasons.
"Disbelief is less often the result of intellectual objections than of the clash
between religious beliefs and attitudes and sensibilities that have been
shaped by an environment that leaves little room for God or the sacred."[4]
These foundational beliefs are, then, pretheoretical. We have acquired them
without thinking about them. And by the time we do think about them (if
we ever do), they are already there.

That does not mean that these foundational notions are not intellectual.
Rather, they are profoundly intellectual in the sense that they can be expressed in propositions, propositions that serve as premises in all the thinking we do. They answer seven basic questions and give us a place to stand
and a place to argue from.

SEVEN BASIC QUESTIONS

1. *What is prime reality—the really real?* To this we might answer God, or the gods, or the material cosmos. Our answer here is the most fundamental. It sets the boundaries for the answers that can consistently be given to the other six questions.

2. *What is the nature of external reality, that is, the world around us?* Here our answers point to whether we see the world as created or autonomous, as chaotic or orderly, as matter or spirit; and whether we emphasize our subjective, personal relationship to the world or its objectivity apart from us.

3. *What is a human being?* To this we might answer: a highly complex machine, a sleeping god, a person made in the image of God, a "naked ape."

4. *What happens to a person at death?* Here we might reply personal extinction, or transformation to a higher state, or reincarnation, or departure to a shadowy existence on "the other side."

5. *Why is it possible to know anything at all?* Sample answers include the idea that we are made in the image of an all-knowing God or that consciousness and rationality developed under the contingencies of survival in a long process of evolution.

6. *How do we know what is right and wrong?* Again, perhaps we are made in the image of a God whose character is good, or right and wrong are determined by human choice alone or what feels good, or the notions simply developed under an impetus toward cultural or physical survival.

7. *What is the meaning of human history?* To this we might answer: to realize the purposes of God or the gods, to make a paradise on earth, to prepare a people for a life in community with a loving and holy God, and so forth.

Today many worldviews are alive and operating in the hearts and minds of people in the United States and other Western nations. We are indeed a pluralist society. But two are especially relevant for our purpose: (1) various varieties of Christian theism (traditional to modern) and (2) naturalism. Here are thumbnail sketches of these two views.[5]

Basic *Christian theism* declares that the most fundamental reality is the tri-une, infinite-personal God of the Bible, who is omnipotent, omniscient and omnipresent, and whose character is absolutely and exhaustively good. God intentionally created the world to be orderly (a uniformity of cause and effect) and open to his own and our reordering. He created human beings in his image (including being personal, morally capable and responsible, and intellectually knowledgeable). Human beings have been created to realize God's ultimate intention to establish his forever family of men and women in a finally perfected kingdom. The pattern of human history involves creation, fall, redemption (the centerpiece of which is Jesus' life, death and resurrection), and glorification (for those who are committed to Jesus Christ) or condemnation (for those who reject him).

Vaguer versions of *theism* retain the notion of an infinite-personal God who creates but are less specific about the character of God, may downplay or reject his triunity, and usually are less specific regarding life after death and God's role in history. This tendency to less specificity historically has led to *deism,* in which God no longer is fully endowed with personhood or even intentionality. In much of modern America, the undermining of traditional theism has resulted in what Christian Smith and Melinda Lundquist Denton call Moralistic Therapeutic Deism, in which God is reduced to a "combination of Divine Butler and Cosmic Therapist."[6]

Naturalism declares that the natural world (matter and energy in a complex, ever-changing form) is the most fundamental reality. There is no God and thus no creation. The entire cosmos, including human beings, has no inherent meaning or significance, only the variety of meanings that human beings give it. Human death is personal extinction. Whatever intelligence or moral character human beings have is the result of their own autonomous invention. The surest form of knowledge comes from the application of the methods of science. Some find this situation challenging but livable and are optimistic about the ultimately futureless life; others struggle or are pessimistic to the point of despair.

As Christians we know how tenaciously we hold our commitment to the existence of the triune God. Such tenacity is also present in one of America's most astute and candid philosophers. Thomas Nagel, a proponent of naturalism, writes in *The Last Word,* a book well worth reading by Christians as a model of insight and honesty: "I want atheism to be true and am made uneasy by the fact that some of the most intelligent and well-informed people I know are religious believers. It isn't just that I don't believe in God and, naturally, hope that I'm right in my belief. It's that I hope there is no God! I don't want the universe to be like that."[7]

To overcome such a commitment to naturalism will take more than a simple change of mind. It will require an intellectual—nay, spiritual— conversion. That the beginning of such a conversion can take place, however, is illustrated by the change of mind—though not spirit—of Antony Flew, perhaps the most famous vocal atheist since Bertrand Russell. In December 2004, he let it be known that while he had not converted to Christianity or even to a fully theistic God, he now believes some sort of impersonal, intelligent God exists.[8]

There is nowhere that naturalism and Christian theism clash more than in Christian thinking related to evolution. Christian apologists, especially those working in intellectual environments such as the university, will inevitably have to address the issue. It is, in fact, one of the five most frequently raised objections to the Christian understanding of reality. The other three are the *problem of evil,* various forms of *relativism* (which will be discussed in the following chapter), the charge that belief in God is *wish fulfillment* (which was briefly treated in chapter three, p. 50) and *exclusivism* (which is taken up in chapter nine). These four can be effectively addressed. But the disagreements over evolution are so fundamental that neither side seems able to see the strength of the other's argument.

While naturalism reigns in U.S. public schools and universities, it is not as popular elsewhere in U.S. society. Gallup polls indicate that only 10 percent of the population is committed to a fully naturalistic version of evolution.[9] Some 40-45 percent believe in a "recent creation" and 40-45 percent in "god-guided" creation. That means that in many contexts, Christians will not face objections arising from naturalistic evolution. Nonetheless, the evolutionary paradigm is so embedded in the American educational system—bottom to top—that it is a major barrier to a fully Christian understanding of reality among both Christians and those who are being invited to Christian faith.

EVOLUTION AND THE NATURALIST WORLDVIEW

The evolutionary theory taught in public schools and universities today accounts for changes in the biosphere without any reference to God or the gods or any transcendent realm. This basically Darwinian (or neo-Darwinian) theory is considered by the entire university community to be certainly true. In the university mind, challenges claiming that evolutionary theory does not actually account for what it pretends to—whether that challenge be sheer skepticism (Michael Denton) or an alternative explanation such as design science (Michael Behe) or "biblical creationism" (Henry Morris)—cannot possibly be true. Nor could any other conceivable challenge be true. Evolution by natural causes is a fact. Nature did it. Okay, we don't know all the details; our theories may need refinement. But evolution is a fact. End of story.

As Sir Julian Huxley said in a lecture in 1959: "In the evolutionary pattern of thought there is no longer either need or room for the supernatural. The earth was not created; it evolved. So did all the animals and plants that inhabit it, including our human selves, mind and soul as well as brain and body. So did religion."[10] Elsewhere and near the same time, Huxley wrote: "The first point to make about Darwin's theory is that it is no longer a theory but a fact. . . . Darwinism has come of age, so to speak. We are no longer having to bother about establishing the fact of evolution."[11] Richard Dawkins echoed this in 1986: "Although atheism might have been *logically* tenable before Darwin, Darwin made it possible to be an intellectually fulfilled atheist."[12]

Evolution has itself become a major element in the modern naturalist's worldview. No matter how flawed or inadequate its explanations may be, today the evolutionary model will always be preferred over any challenges. The common assumption is that human beings not only can, but already have, come to understand much about how the universe was formed and how it "evolved" from its origin in a singularity to its elaboration into its present state. We are here as the result of a long string of undesigned, naturally caused developments.

If we can explain how we as human beings have arisen from inanimate nature, we can explain the most complex aspect of reality there is. Naturalism is therefore a true worldview. The "fact" of evolution becomes the justification for naturalism as a worldview. Naturalism thus reigns as the dominant worldview of the university.

Actually, the argument takes two forms. One starts by seeming to demonstrate that the biosphere has evolved by natural causes and concludes that naturalism is true. The other starts by assuming the truth of naturalism, then concludes that evolution is a fact.

Argument 1. The appearance of human beings with all their unique characteristics of rational thought, compassion, aesthetic creativity and moral capacity has seemed to be the most difficult phenomenon to account for without calling on a divine personal cause. Since Darwin (and now with much more reason than Darwin) it can be shown that known natural causes are sufficient to have brought about the current state of the biosphere—including the appearance of human beings. No supernatural cause is required to explain the existence of the most complex form of reality, the biosphere. Therefore, God does not exist, and naturalism is true.

Strictly speaking, this argument is a non sequitur. That is, the conclusion does not follow from the premises. That God is not required to explain the existence of the universe or life does not require that God not exist. God could exist without there being any reason we could know. He could exist for the simple reason that he exists; after all, in the theistic sense God is self-existent and needs no further fact to explain his existence. He just is what it is to be. He needs no other reason than himself. Dawkins can declare that naturalistic evolution allows him to be a fulfilled atheist, but there is no reason for him to do so. Even if all the causes for the changes in the biosphere could be shown to be natural, God might well exist as the ultimate cause of these so-called natural causes. Logically, one simply cannot prove such a negative. So Dawkins's ultimate belief that there is no God requires as much commitment as the belief of a theist.

Argument 2. Naturalism is so embedded in the university world as an assumption that the truth of evolution need not be argued.[13] God does not exist. The biosphere came into existence a long time ago and developed to its present state; evolution (i.e., development, complexification of the biosphere) has occurred. There are no other causes than natural causes. In other words, naturalistic, undesigned evolution is a fact.

This argument is at least valid. If God or some equally transcendent reality does not exist, then only natural causes are available to account for anything at all (the universe, life or the morning paper).

These two arguments can be found today among both scientists and nonscientists. They intertwine, sometimes as circular reasoning, but often appearing to reinforce each other.

Christians, however, are committed to the notion that there is an infinite-personal God who created the world and us in his image. We—and I include myself here—do not need to be committed to any particular version of how God created. But the notion that God intentionally created the world because he wanted to is at the heart of the Bible and the Christian worldview. So is the notion that we have learned this by revelation from God in Scripture written by his chosen prophets. We do not need to be committed to a particular interpretation of how the Scripture relates to scientific explanation. We should be committed to believe whatever it is that Scripture teaches, but our interpretations, as accurate as they may well be, are still subject to error and to correction. Whatever conflict there may be is not between the Bible and science but between our theology and scientific theory.

The result is that some Christians are *biblical creationists,* who read the Bible as if it contained scientific information and conclude that God created the earth in seven days of twenty-four hours each only a few thousand years ago.[14] Some Christians are *theistic evolutionists,* who believe that God created the universe billions of years ago largely in the way accounted for by astrophysics and modern biology but by God's design and intention, not by mere chance and necessity. A newer breed of Christians are advocates of *design science*. They are content to point out the fatal flaws in evolutionary theory and propose, rather modestly, that the existence of design in the universe (and therefore some sort of designer) is a better explanation of the same set of physical facts that evolutionary theory uses to justify its claim to truth; moreover, they say, it accounts for a host of facts that cannot be accounted for by evolutionary theory. Finally, there are those like myself, just plain *Christian theists* who believe the universe was created by God but are not committed to a specific version of how it came to be in its current form.

In the present intellectual environment, the claims and arguments of both the biblical creationists and the design scientists—no matter how strong they are—usually fail even to get a hearing. Given naturalistic premises, on the surface of it they can't be true. Theistic evolutionists and Christian theists who are uncertain about the details do not face quite the same problem. Both can challenge the underlying naturalism of Darwinian evolution without challenging its mechanism.[15] But a student, for example, who tries in a modern university classroom to raise questions sparked by either biblical creationism or design science will at best be tolerated; at worst he or she will be laughed at by both teachers and fellow students, ridiculed minimally for being intellectually incompetent or ridiculed maximally as a threat to the university and to rationality itself. Dawkins illustrates this well. He says, "It is absolutely safe to say that if you meet somebody who claims not to believe in evolution, that person is ignorant, stupid, or insane (or wicked, but I'd rather not consider that)."[16]

Take the case of a first-year student at the University of Texas. A group of dean's scholars in the College of Natural Sciences were meeting weekly with two professors (math and computer science) over a brown-bag lunch. This day I was presenting a paper on Lewis Thomas, whose views cross the border between naturalism and panentheism. The discussion was exciting, one of the most exhilarating of my many campus forays. An hour into the discus-

sion, one woman said, "You'll probably laugh at me, but I am a creationist."
Laugh? The computer scientist exploded. "What a harebrained idea! Of
all the ideas to believe, why that one? It's unspeakable."

A couple of other Christians and I tried to soften the blow to her ego, but
such putdowns can wreak a lot of damage to a young mind in the formative
stage. Moreover, they stifle dialogue in the pursuit of truth.

Both biblical creationists and theistic evolutionists have been around
since Darwin. The former make their case on the basis of a particular hermeneutic of Scripture that is not universally held by Christians. Many evangel-
icals are reticent for theological reasons to read the Bible as a book of science. Such a method of reading the Bible has not had, nor I think ever will
have, any impact on the university world.

Design science, however, has begun to be recognized as a small player on
a very large field.[17] People like biologist Michael Behe, mathematician-
philosopher William Dembski and law professor Phillip E. Johnson (whose
specialty is argumentation) have gotten the attention of publicly vocal evolutionists like Dawkins and the late Stephen Jay Gould. Design science is still
on the margin of academic discourse, but it is at least a player. Its arguments
are being weighed by scientists in the mainstream.[18] Still, it remains to be
seen if the prior commitment to the truth of naturalism—there is no God—
will be brought into serious doubt in the academy.[19]

Design science may have some very powerful and academically respect-
able arguments, but in the end these may cause no more than a temporary
ripple in the vast sea of naturalistic evolution. What is at stake, as Johnson
has pointed out, is the dominance of naturalism as a worldview in the academy. He has pictured this worldview as a huge ship that is springing leaks
and will inevitably sink even as those on board are celebrating their dominance by dining on cheese and wine. We wait to see.[20]

In the meantime, what is an apologist to do? A huge barrier is raised by
the recalcitrance of the university mind. It must be breached or avoided.
How can that happen?

I must admit at this point that I have no idea how a biblical creationist can do either. I find the notion of a twenty-four-hour creation as unlikely to be true as do the full-fledged naturalists. I realize that this very admission may prevent some readers from reading further in this book. It is easy for us as Christians to be just as stubborn as our counterparts in the non-Christian world. But please, please, stay with me for at least the next few paragraphs. To stop reading here would only serve to illustrate my major thesis in this chapter: that some positions on evolution have become so embedded in the heart that no information, no argument will shake them. We must, as Christians, take care about which of our faith commitments really belong at this "given" or "pretheoretical" or "utterly committed" level. Not to listen to those with whom we fundamentally disagree is not only to deem their beliefs untrue but to denigrate their dignity as human beings made in the image of God. So please, do stick with me as I explain my position. Consider whether it has any merit, and disagree with me then, if you find it doesn't.

Without going into any detail, here are the two main reasons that I am unable to suggest any way for a biblical creationist to engage a typical naturalist who believes in evolution through totally natural causes. First, there is a massive amount of scientific evidence—from astrophysics, geology, paleontology, biology—pointing to an ancient origin of both the universe and the earth. Second, it is by no means necessary to read the accounts in Genesis 1 and 2 as containing any scientific information at all. I have become convinced that these accounts were written to counter the mythologies of the ancient world—Egyptian, Mesopotamian, Chaldean, Canaanite—and to provide the Israelites with a solid antimythological grasp of the infinite-personal God as the foundation of reality. They have nothing to do with modern theories of either astrophysics or biology.[21] As C. S. Lewis once commented, "The kind of truth we are often demanding was, in my opinion, not even envisaged by the ancients."[22] I can understand why biblical creationists hold their view, and I respect them for the strength of their conviction because I know it comes from a desire to honor our common Lord and Savior. But I do not find their views at all convincing.

But what about the Christians who hold the other views? Perhaps my answer to this question may surprise almost all my readers. In general, I believe that in their witness to their Christian faith most Christians should never raise the issue of evolution. They should talk about it only if they cannot avoid doing so.

Of course, every Christian should be ready to answer questions when these are raised. We all need to know enough about the topic to make a credible response. (See the bibliography on pp. 174-77 for suggestions.) But deliberately raising the issue will most likely lead to long and futile argument. Of course, a good case can be made to bring Darwinism into doubt. Nonetheless, such arguments are highly complex and demand a knowledge of biology, biochemistry, genetics, geology and philosophy that is rarely to be found even among professional apologists. Even if you have a profound knowledge of evolutionary theory, you will often face one of two situations. Either your interlocutor will reject your judgment because you personally are not a biologist (and thus not a credible authority), or he or she will have so little grasp of the issues that they will not understand your profound explanations. The upshot is that in our witness we should usually focus on other topics.

As contenders for the Christian faith, we need to be clear about why we are addressing evolution at all.[23] The universe has undergone modification since its beginning. That's a fact. Most Christians can agree to that. The issue is how this modification came about: was it with or without the engagement of God? Naturalism, not evolution, is the enemy. So unless one goes to great length to be educated about evolution at a profound level—by reading not just the Christian critics but the biologists and other experts who believe the biosphere came into its present state by totally natural and undesigned means—it is best to leave the dialogue to the Christian experts.

Some Christian apologists have been using the insights of intelligent design as a wedge to trigger doubt in those committed to naturalistic evolution. They will not approve my recommendation that most Christians shun the topic of evolution in the presentation of the gospel. To be fair to their point of view, I have included an extended rejoinder likely to be shared by most of them (see the following footnote).[24]

Christians like myself can appeal to the Behes, the Dembskis and the Johnsons rather than trying to deal in depth with the issue. We should want people to believe in Jesus as Lord and Savior far more than we want them to doubt Darwinian evolution. In fact, some form of theistic evolution is still the dominant position of Christians who are scientists. They are satisfied to say that the universe and the biosphere may have changed largely along the paths outlined by Darwinian evolution. They reject, however, that this process was without design at the most fundamental level. God did it, they say. How he did it is not important. William Edgar sums it up well: "It is best to let the Bible speak on its own terms and not force particular scientific theories out of it. It is best also to let science do its work, occasionally reminding scientists that they cannot claim neutrality."[25]

Notice that we have been considering arguments that are needed to counter the reigning worldview of the public schools and universities. What about the public at large? Here, as noted earlier, some 40-50 percent already believe in a "recent creation" and 40-45 percent in "god-guided" creation. That means that outside of academic settings, those who speak for the faith will only rarely face objections from the standpoint of naturalistic evolution.

If we choose to do battle with evolution, the temptation will be for us to give inadequate explanations of what the evolutionists teach and encourage an attitude of "how stupid must be the evolutionists to believe such tripe!" In doing so, we will only give evolutionists further evidence that we Christians are benighted ignoramuses—just as they have always thought.

Let us let the whole issue of evolution remain unaddressed, therefore, except when it arises as a question. Then let's keep our answer short and defer to Christian experts for detail. There are far more central issues to consider. Not the least of which is relativism, to which we now turn.

8

WHO AM I TO JUDGE?

Worldviews and Relativism

In the 1950s, when I was an undergraduate, the most persistent objection to the Christian faith was that it simply was not true. This was expressed in a variety of ways. "Jesus was not resurrected. The stories about this are myths or legends. If he lived at all, he died and stayed dead." "What God wants of us—if there even is a God—is to live a good life. It's not true that we must acknowledge Jesus Christ as Lord and Savior." In short, belief in Christ was considered irrational.

Today, the very notions of rationality and truth are under attack. Even science's attempt to discover the truth about nature is brought into question. For some radical postmodernists, scientific theories are neither true nor false. They are rather "stories" or "descriptions" that scientists have agreed on because when they are used they achieve the right results.

Granted, among most practicing scientists and people in general water is still hydrogen and oxygen, two parts to one. Ordinary material reality is still seen to be governed by the category of objective truth. But in matters of morality and religion there really is no truth. Or, rather, there are many truths, and these truths may contradict each other. "What's true for me doesn't have to be true for you" is the common way this is expressed. Or: "Who am I to judge?"

The story of how this shift in cultural consciousness has come about is interesting but unnecessary to tell here.[1] Suffice it to say that when naturalism declared that there is nothing outside the material world, it released the human mind from any responsibility to a transcendent God or any influence from him. It left the mind on its own and gave human reason its autonomy. As one teenager said, God is there "for somebody to talk to and help us through our problems. Of course, he doesn't talk back."[2] We can think and do pretty much whatever we want.

THE AUTONOMY OF REASON

While this movement away from traditional Christian theism freed the human mind from any external restraint, it left it with a host of problems. The most significant questions can no longer be answered by human reason. Am I just a material being? What, if anything, makes me valuable? Why am I here? What should I live for? How should I treat my fellow human beings—the family next door, the people in my village or city, those who live in my country and, then, other countries? There are many contradictory answers to these questions. Often the different answers lead to conflict. How can we get along given our deepest differences? Why should we even try?

Perhaps the most troubling question of all is, Why should I trust the workings of my own mind when it is completely impersonal, unwitting, undesigned matter in motion?

Naturalists have tried to find a foundation for answering those questions. But they have failed. Without a transcendent standard of reference, all we have is our own desire, our own personal opinion or our own social custom to rely on.

FROM PLURALISM TO RELATIVISM

The social fact of *pluralism* has lead to the theoretical principle of *relativism*—relativism of every kind: moral, religious, philosophical, even—in postmodern form—scientific. Truth itself has become personal opinion.

It is especially troubling that, along with adherents to other religious views, many Christians have been swept along with the cultural flow. There is no reason for serious Christians to be relativists, but many who otherwise claim to be Christians have either lost their earlier exclusive commitment to Christ or have never understood that it is a part of biblical faith. They commend religious belief but are not concerned with which religion it is.[3]

The depth of penetration of this worldview commitment to relativism is fully and painfully illustrated in *Soul Searching*, a recent study of the "religious and spiritual lives of American teenagers." Sociologists Christian Smith and Melinda Lundquist Denton analyze the results of in-depth interviews of 267 teenagers and conclude that religious relativism is the pervasive background assumption of most teens who identify themselves as Christian. Take, example, this interview with a fifteen-year-old Native American Catholic from Illinois. He maintained that "God was present in the desk, trees, and grass." Then he was asked about others who take a different view of God:

> T *[Teen]: I couldn't say anything. It's their opinion. I have my own opinion.*
>
> I *[Interviewer]: Are you right?*
>
> T: *Ah, I don't know. I have no idea, but.*
>
> I: *Is there a right or wrong answer when it comes to God?*
>
> T: *There is no right answer.*
>
> I: *Why not?*
>
> T: *There isn't any wrong answer. 'Cause it's God, you can't prove, it's just what you believe.*[4]

Smith and Denton comment:

> *When each individual has his or her own unique and self-authenticating experiences and felt needs and desires, it is impossible for any other (alien) individual to properly evaluate or judge those chosen beliefs, commitments, desires, or lifestyle. The typical bywords, rather, are "Who am I to judge?" "If that's what they choose, whatever," "Each person decides for himself," and "If it works for them, fine."*[5]

They do, however, have one word of hope, and it is enough to give us courage: "In fact, despite the rhetoric, few teenagers actually consistently sustain such radical relativism. In certain ways and areas of life, teens do actually draw clear lines, often quite moralistic lines."[6] In other words, teens— and adults too—cannot actually live by radical relativism. It is this fact that leaves an opening for effective arguments.

Relativism has ramifications in every area of life (social, political, religious, technical, entertainment, manufacturing and the marketplace) and at every level (from individual to international). But because we are dealing here with Christian witness, I will focus only on the religious situation.

RESPONDING TO RELIGIOUS RELATIVISM

When we witness to the truth of the gospel or argue for a particular view of Jesus or God, the response is something like this: "Well, that's okay for you, but I don't believe that. I believe this." For example, you believe that there is a resurrection of the body, and after death either a blissful life in heaven with God and his people or an unhappy continued personal existence apart from God in hell. But your neighbor believes that conscious life just ends at death. Down the street is a New Ager who believes he will be reincarnated. Still both of them say, "It's nice that you believe what you do. I don't, but that's okay." Here, then, are three mutually incompatible views: resurrection, extinction and reincarnation.

If a person says each one is true for whoever believes it, then unless this "orientation of the heart" is changed, no rational apologetic can proceed. The Christian apologist has three options: to cease arguing, to confront the commitment to relativism or to make an end run. Obviously, a Christian should not give up. Let's take each of the other options in turn.

Confrontation. Relativism itself can be confronted by pointing out its implications. For example, for all three views of life after death to be true at the same time, the world would have to be contradictory place. It would have to be the case (1) that human beings are "created infinities" (that is, made by God for eternal fellowship with God), (2) that human beings are solely material beings that cease to exist when their bodies fall apart and (3) that human beings are "sparks of the divine" who move back and forth between material embodiments—today you are Joan; after death and reincarnation you (or what you have become) are Jack, Jill, Juan, etc., etc.

This situation is simply impossible. Any one of these three alternatives could be the case, or a further alternative could be the case, but they cannot all be the way things are. That would require a universe with no structural consistency; it would be a chaos, not a cosmos. Nor could a person's belief make any one of these eventualities true. Still, people often seem to think so. That is, some people believe that what happens to you at death depends on what you believe. Your belief determines your destiny. But to think that a person's personal belief about the afterlife could make that belief true, as I have heard some students suggest, has nothing to recommend it at all. When does what one believes about the physical world make any difference at all to what that world actually is? We can't make our dreams come true just by dreaming them. Nor can we make our beliefs come true just by believing them. I dream, no, I believe "she loves me"—but everyone else can see she doesn't!

A more sophisticated form of religious pluralism bordering on relativism says that while religions contradict each other here on earth, in the final analysis they are all different cultural expressions of the same incomprehensible God. While this has been argued at length by John Hick and other theologians, it has several very obvious flaws.[7] First, as Hick recognizes, each of these religions actually is different. Some call for the violent elimination of those who disagree with them simply because they disagree; others call for respect and tolerance; others insist that one might well die for one's faith but never kill—and so forth. But that is just the point: it is these differences on the local level that we must deal with.

Second, the view that all religions are the same because they are all expressions of the same incomprehensible God is itself simply another religion. It has made the situation more, not less, plural.

Third, if God really is incomprehensible, then none of the religions are revelations of who he, she or it is. By being concrete, these religions have defined the indefinable. If God is ineffable, then nothing said about God could in any way be a revelation. Beliefs about God would simply be human constructs, one no more true or false than any other. In any case, such relativism, no matter how sophisticated, will not help us live with our deepest differences.

In the final analysis, as human beings we need the truth. Aristotle once said, "All men by nature desire to know [the truth]."[8] We may not know the truth, but only the truth will satisfy our needs not only for personal but for social peace.

I have found this method of directly addressing relativism to be quite effective.[9] Still, after a lecture explaining this in some detail, it is almost inevitable that one or more students will object. Sometimes they do so regardless of how I explain relativism's incoherence or detail its impossibility of being true.

A CASE IN POINT: SWARTHMORE COLLEGE

Take a case at Swarthmore College, September 1991. In a "Ten Myths" program to clarify the Christian faith, Christian students put up a large poster display proclaiming that the notion that "It doesn't matter what you believe. All religions are basically the same" is a myth. The campus community went into an uproar. Some called for the removal of the poster. In an ensuing meeting with the deans who tried to deal with the controversy, the leader of the Christian group was asked to explain what she believed. She responded and focused her answer on the uniqueness of Christ.

One dean then said, "Well, it's obvious to me that people who believe what you do don't belong here."

Two days later three Christian leaders met again with three deans. Here is a direct quotation from a report later made by the Christian group:

Potentially explosive situation. The threat to "shut down" 10 MYTHS still remains. We appeal to freedom of speech rights and propose that if we have violated any campus policy or anyone's rights then "please show us where." Deans agree that we have done neither but go on to point out that our beliefs in Jesus as the only way to God inherently "demean and depersonalize other

people." Agreement is reached to let 10 MYTHS continue. Sometime in the
discussion a dean angrily speaks what is an enormous irony: "Can't you all
see that Swarthmore College has prided itself for over 100 years on being a
place of tolerance!"[10]

This is, of course, ironic, because there is always allowance for some absolutists to have a significant forum, at least in the university: I am thinking of feminists, exponents of alternate sexuality and Marxists (and free-market exponents, too) who teach explicitly and evangelistically from those points of view. Each academic discipline tends as well to have "orthodoxies," some of them passing fads with the power of an "orthodoxy." Deconstruction in literary theory is an example.

But there are deeper troubles for relativism than these ironies. The whole notion is, I believe, incorrect. Relativism as it is expressed on campus, in hallways and dorm rooms, and in classrooms and learned papers is ultimately incoherent. One does not have to evaluate relativism from the standpoint of any particular absolutist position to see that this is so. The rationality of relativism itself collapses under examination. The only problem is that those whose relativism has achieved a pretheoretical status often fail to recognize the collapse.

Making an end run. There is another way to address the dominant relativism of our culture. That is to make an end run. If our opponent's linebacker keeps our halfback from running straight up the middle, we can try an end run or perhaps a pass. As Smith and Denton have already suggested, few people really live by radical relativism. So instead of confronting relativism itself, one who defends Christian faith can correctly assume that people actually act as if there is a difference between true and false religious views. It is only when people are confronted with religious ideas or moral norms that they don't like that they spout the cultural cliché "What's true for you doesn't have to be true for me."

Here's one way to do an end run.[11] Ask a person (or a group) to list the reasons that people believe the way they do. They will respond with a host of factors—sociological, psychological, authoritarian, philosophical. Then ask them which of those factors are good reasons. It will take them little time to reject as a good reason the one most often cited—people believe what they were taught as children. They will also soon tell you that believing like their peers or even their entire culture is what people do but that it is not a good reason. They will soon see, too, that psychological reasons (it feels good; it gives me what I want) are not good ones. Authority figures—priests, gurus, politicians, professors—will soon be rejected.

When they are asked why these are not good reasons, they will say things like "Well, my parents—my friends, my society, my culture—could be wrong," or "The priest just wants people to come to church," or "What I want maybe I shouldn't have." What these answers reveal, of course, is that when push comes to shove, everyone uses the category of *truth* to make their decisions. The apologist can then ask, "How can you tell when something is true?" Those present may already have listed such criteria as consistency, coherence, best explanation of all the evidence—historical, scientific, personal. Even if you have to remind them of these factors, they will usually see that they are indeed relevant to a justified belief.

This procedure puts Christians and the people they address onto the same playing field. Truth is then an issue. One can make sense of the differences between various understandings of life after death, and the case for and against each can proceed.

THE DEPTH OF WORLDVIEW COMMITMENT

Every attempt should, of course, be made to bridge the presuppositional gap between apologist and skeptic. Nonetheless, some will still be unshakably recalcitrant. So committed are they to some form of religious relativism that no amount of explanation or argument will move them. Philosophers such as Richard Rorty and theologians such as John Hick have argued for highly sophisticated forms of relativism. Yet their arguments are, in the final analysis, no more compelling than the simple relativism of first-year college students. Moreover, the incoherence and inconsistency of their views have been pointed out in great detail in a sophistication equal to or more than their original arguments.[12] Still, they do not change their minds. Why?

I once asked a prominent theologian why this was the case. He pushed my question aside as if either it was stupid or the answer was obvious. I don't think either is the case. When someone who is otherwise intelligent does not see that 2 + 2 = 4, something very odd must be going on. One explanation is given by political philosopher J. Budziszewski. He suggests that it is due to the "postmodern predilection for obscure language"[13]: "C. S. Lewis said that a good test of whether you understand something is whether you can express it in uneducated language, in street talk. . . . The problem is not a lack of education or of intellectual capacity. The problem is that once postmodernism is translated into street talk, anyone can see how silly it is."[14] Budziszewski insists that he has never met a postmodernist who could do that.

Obfuscation can indeed prevent clear self-perception. But I think that the problem goes deeper than this. Relativism and evolution are themselves worldview-level ideas. They are not just intellectual readouts of deeper commitments. They are themselves deep commitments.

Nowhere is this more obvious than in Rorty's introduction to *Philosophy and Social Hope*. Rorty is a philosopher who often writes in what Budziszewski calls street language. From his own postmodern position Rorty gladly admits that he does not know how to argue for his own positions or against those of his opponents. Rather, he says, "I suspect that all that either side can do is restate its case over and over again, in context after context. . . . The controversy [between my view and others] . . . is too radical to permit of being judged from some neutral standpoint."[15]

This is, it seems to me, a counsel of despair. It means that what really determines what people come to believe or what actually causes them to change their minds is some form of cultural power—rhetoric, or charisma, or forceful coercion of metanarratives or worldviews by those with political or physical power. Might—of various kinds, mind you, not just political or physical—makes right. Surely philosophy, theology and politics have not come down to this lowest common denominator. What is the difference, then, between Rorty's liberal democracy brought about by a reign of rhetoric and Vladimir Lenin's socialism prompted by a reign of terror? If Rorty's philosophy were to begin to reign in the hearts of a significant portion of our culture, God's common grace may be all we have to rely on to prevent the tyranny of those "strong poets" who can get us to talk the way they want us to.

There is at least one form of Buddhism that includes these two fundamental notions: (1) ultimate reality is not only unexpressible but unknowable, and (2) nonviolence is the ultimate ethical principle. If (1) is true, then ethics has no foundation except in human imagination, which itself has no ontological foundation. In short, if (1) is true, (2) has no ground. On the other hand, if (2) is true, (1) is false; ultimate reality does have some intellectual content. As nearly as I can tell, both (1) and (2) characterize some forms of Buddhism at its most sophisticated level.[16]

Following Rorty's postmodern principle, however, one cannot have and does not need a consistent worldview. One needs only a narrative that works long enough to keep human beings alive long enough to continue to propagate. At this point in Western culture, evolution and relativism still have survival value. But who knows for how long!

Of course, other fundamental commitments also prevent the "hearing" of a case for Christian faith. Philosopher Roy Clouser gives two examples of a commitment to an overall pure secularism: "A fellow graduate student once said to me, 'Show me that any belief I have is religious and I'll give it up on the spot.' And a faculty colleague once commented that the only way religion should be taught is 'with great hostility.'"[17]

Harvard zoologist Richard Lewontin displays a similar commitment to materialism, which Victor Reppert characterizes as "a scientific form of fideism":

Our willingness to accept scientific claims that are against common sense is the key to an understanding of the real struggle between science and the supernatural. We take the side of science in spite of the patent absurdity of some of its constructs, of its failure to fulfill many of its extravagant promises of health and life, in spite of the tolerance of the scientific community of unsubstantiated just-so stories because we have a prior commitment, a commitment to materialism. It is not that the methods and institutions of science somehow compel us to accept a material explanation of the phenomenal world, but, on the contrary, that we are forced by our a priori adherence to material causes to create an apparatus of investigation and a set of concepts that produce material explanations, no matter how counterintuitive, no matter how mystifying to the uninitiated. Moreover, that materialism is absolute, for we cannot allow a Divine Foot in the door. The eminent Kant scholar Lewis Beck used to say that anyone who could believe in God could believe in anything. To appeal to an omnipotent deity is to allow that at any moment the regularities of nature may be ruptured, that miracles may happen.[18]

Try getting a person so fully committed even to consider the possibility that there is anything supernatural about reality!

Christians simply need to acknowledge that rational Christian arguments will not of themselves persuade. Maybe this is a good thing. At least it keeps Christians from claiming the power and authority of the Holy Spirit.

9

THE HEART WANTS WHAT IT WANTS

Moral Blindness

Moral blindness vies with worldviews for pride of position as the most prevalent reason for the failure of good arguments to persuade. If the worldview factor goes to the heart of our pretheoretical but nonetheless intellectual commitments, moral blindness goes to the heart of our human rebellion against God. Sometimes, of course, both the human mind and the human heart will play us for fools and blackguards. Let us see how we are often belied by our own selfish heart.

THE MORAL BLINDNESS PRINCIPLE

> **Christian claims to truth often imply moral obligation. As ordinary human beings, we do not want to be morally obligated, and so we reject ideas that obligate us.**

Take for example one strong claim of Jesus. On the night of his arrest, Jesus told his disciples, "I am the way, and the truth, and the life. No one comes to the Father except through me" (Jn 14:6). This statement, startling to many today, rankles nonbelievers for at least two reasons.

First, if it is true, it is not just a truth about Jesus himself; it is a truth about us and our eternal future. It means that in order to have eternal life with God, we must "go through Jesus." That is, we must pay attention to what he demands of us, whatever that is. When we listen to him, we soon learn that he wants such total submission that we will have to radically reorder our life. We will have to be willing to change how we live now if we are to be with him after we die. The alternative is eternal death—eternal separation from all that makes life worth living.

Second, Jesus' statement goes against the current idea that everyone has a right to his or her own religion, that people should be able to pick and choose what they believe about God and salvation. The Christian claim here is too exclusive. In modern parlance, we are supposed to be *tolerant*, and that means we are not to claim that any religious view is false, even if it contradicts our own which we believe to be true. Religious truths are relative to a particular person, society, culture and time.

If we claim that Jesus is the only way to God, we are hurting people's feelings or perhaps even oppressing the people themselves. We should either abandon our exclusive faith or, at a minimum, keep our opinions to ourselves. Of course, we cannot do this and be followers of our Lord. We have already seen how the precommitment to relativism is a barricade to effective rational argument. Here we will examine how the exclusive claims of Christianity pose a moral problem.

It is certainly no wonder that people find Jesus' words too demanding. Their truth grates against the grain of our selfish nature. We don't want the truth to be true, so we reject it. Then the truth we have rejected appears false to us, and we may even come to hate it. Many people hate the truth of John 14:6.

Long ago Augustine recognized the profound psychological/moral/intellectual perversion that is involved in coming to hate the truth. "Why does truth call forth hatred?" Augustine asked. Then he answered:

> *Simply because truth is loved in such a way that those who love some other thing want it to be the truth, and precisely because they do not wish to be deceived, are unwilling to be convinced that they are indeed being deceived.*

Thus they hate the truth for the sake of that other thing which they love, be-cause they take it for the truth. They love truth when it enlightens them, they hate it when it accuses them.[1]

A fascinating illustration of this phenomenon occurred in early 2003:

During the invasion of Iraq, the Iraqi Minister of Information appeared daily before a bank of microphones to repeat over and over again: "There are no American infidels in Baghdad! Never!" This as American soldiers were taking over government buildings a few blocks away. Presuming that the minister was not simply lying, he was being utterly, unshakably consistent in the face of contrary evidence.[2]

The point is that truth can stare us in the face, and we—even with our desire to know the truth—can not only reject it but also come to hate it. John Stackhouse gives another example of the moral barrier: "Woody Allen . . . incurred the wrath of public opinion when he began a romantic relationship with his adopted daughter. In the face of unrelenting criticism as his behavior contravened most North Americans' sense of morality, he famously declared, 'The heart wants what it wants.'"[3]

Throughout his ministry and especially toward the end, Jesus felt the brunt of those who claimed to be pursuing the truth but instead were seeking to justify their own beliefs and actions.

Again they came to Jerusalem. As he was walking in the temple, the chief priests, the scribes, and the elders came to him and said, "By what authority are you doing these things [various healings, for example]? . . ." Jesus said to them, "I will ask you one question; answer me, and I will tell you by what authority I do these things. Did the baptism of John come from heaven, or was it of human origin? Answer me." They argued with one another, "If we say 'From heaven,' he will say, 'Why then did you not believe him?' But shall we say 'Of human origin'?"—they were afraid of the crowd, for all regarded

John as truly a prophet. So they answered Jesus, "We do not know." And Jesus said to them, "Neither will I tell you by what authority I am doing these things." (Mk 11:27-33)

Jesus made the religious authorities reveal whether they were seriously seeking the truth before he would tell them what it was. The principle is clear: In the long run only those who do the truth they hear will "hear" the truth. Honesty or integrity is a prerequisite for coming to know.

Note how deeply into the mind and psyche the moral consequences plunge. Paul says that when those who know the truth suppress it, not only is their senseless mind darkened but their moral character is destroyed as well (Rom 1:18-32). Rejecting the truth has horrendous results.

A WARNING

There is, however, a problem with this explanation. If someone rejects—or is not convinced by—a given argument, we may be tempted to attribute this rejection to willful moral blindness. It lets us off the hook. *My argument is good,* I say to myself; *it's my friend who is not.*

But before we draw this conclusion, we should pause. Perhaps our argument *is* flawed. Perhaps our use of it has been inept. Perhaps there is a valid reason why the argument should not be persuasive. Maybe our unconvinced friend has heard exclusive claims before. What about those who have been drawn into heretical cults? Some people have been psychologically scarred by believing their often exclusive claims. Some who have reeled away from abusive cults are often in this position. The swami has failed them; maybe Jesus will too.

Moreover, Jesus did not make the specific, boldly exclusive statement of John 14:6 to anyone who was not already a believer. Even Judas had left before these words were uttered at the Last Supper. When Jesus made his stellar claims about himself in public, he often accompanied them with a direct demonstration of his divine character, often a physical healing or a casting out of demons.[4]

In today's world, a rational justification for believing that Jesus is the only way to God will include much more than the fact that he made the claim. Just how much evidence and argument are enough to justify the claim is moot. Who can know? All one can do is the best one can with what one knows and what one can come to know through further study of the Gospels and prayer.

The conclusion that any given person who refuses to accept our arguments is morally at fault should generally be kept to ourselves. Accusing someone of this fault—even when it is true—can easily be counterproductive. It should be done only with great care and after great prayer.

Still, such a challenge was effective at least once. At a student conference in northern California, I presented a case for the close relationship between belief and obedience based on an exposition of John 7–8. One of those attending realized that precisely this connection was not being made by one of his friends. So, back on campus of Chico State University, he met his friend and laid out the argument from John. The argument worked, and his friend moved from an intellectual acknowledgment that Jesus was Lord to active acceptance and new life in Christ.

Nonetheless, our search for nonrational explanations of the failure of our arguments to persuade needs to be carried out very cautiously. Nancy Pearcey recounts that after her conversion she was beset by doubts arising from her study of sociology. She says,

> *I sought the advice of one of the [Christian] group leaders [on campus], asking desperately for some intellectual tools for defending the notion that there is genuine, objective truth. . . . His response was to steer the conversation out of intellectual territory and into familiar spiritual territory: "Nancy, it sounds like you're having a problem with assurance of salvation."*[5]

He was wrong. He needed to give an honest answer to an honest question. He didn't; perhaps he couldn't. Christians need great sensitivity to the person who is asking the question. A response like "Why do you ask?"

would have revealed that the issue was intellectual and needed an intellectual answer. If the student leader feared that he would be unable to address such an issue, he could have let Pearcey know he was unable and help her find someone who could.

RESPONDING TO MORAL BLINDNESS

With proper caution, however, there are ways to respond to evidence of moral blindness. First, we must recognize the lack of honesty in the one asking the question. After one of my public lectures, someone will often stand up and ask what I call a let's-see-if-I-can-stump-the-speaker-and-show-the-audience-I'm-smarter question. InterVarsity evangelist Mark Slaughter calls them "stump the chump" questions. They come so frequently to Christian speakers that, especially given the tone of voice in which they are expressed, it is fairly easy to detect them. Here are a few.

> *"You say God is omnipotent. So could he make a stone so heavy he could not lift it?"*
> *"You say the stories in the Bible are true history. So where did Cain get his wife?"*
> *"Are you telling me that everyone who disagrees with you is going to hell?"*

Of course these questions could be honest.[6] They can and do puzzle people. But often they are thrown out just to heckle or provide a platform for the objector.

The first way to respond is to treat the objector as if he or she were being honest. I heard Francis A. Schaeffer respond this way many times. I really wonder if he ever did anything else. Someone in the audience would raise an objection that on the surface had little merit or relevance to the issues at hand. Schaeffer, however, would treat the question as honest. His answers were themselves highly intelligent. He would find a way not only to make the question relevant but to advance the case for the Christian faith. Sometimes a follow-up question—just as dishonest—would come from the audience, and Schaeffer would treat it in the same way. The result was amazing. Not only would the audience see that Schaeffer was kinder, gentler and more honest than the questioner, but so would the questioner himself (yes, it usually was a him). In this way the gospel got a better hearing with the irrelevant question than without it.

The only time I saw this approach fail to work was in a television interview in Chicago with Irv Kupcinet. After one or two relevant questions and return comments from Schaeffer, Kupcinet said, "But you believe in an historical Adam and Eve, don't you?" This question came out of the blue, having no relevance whatsoever to anything Schaeffer was addressing in his Chicago lectures or anything that had preceded it in the interview. It was calculated to make Schaeffer look dumb. And when Schaeffer took it as an honest question and was given only a couple of sentences to respond, the ploy worked. Frankly, Schaeffer came off looking like a dumb, backwater, fundamentalist idiot. Nonetheless, I think it is a moot point whether Schaeffer should have called Kupcinet's bluff by saying something like "Yes, but what does that have to do with what we were discussing?" A short TV interview is inherently hostile to serious dialogue.

The second way to respond to questions is, indeed, to do so with a question. The answer you get sometimes reveals not only whether the questioner is seeking the truth but where they are in their spiritual life. Jesus was especially adept at this, as we have seen in the example above (pp. 119-20) where the questioners were dishonest.

Philosopher J. Budziszewski is a strong advocate of blowing away the smokescreens of dishonest or self-deceiving questions.

> *When confronted with moral confusions such as relativism, we must distinguish between honest intellectual difficulties, on the one hand, and evasions and self-deceptions on the other. . . . When we fail to recognize . . . smokescreens and suppose that they are honest difficulties, our fine intellectual responses merely allow the people with whom we are speaking opportunities to play further intellectual games.*[7]

Budziszewski believes, as I do, that morality is so ingrained in human nature that we cannot live without wittingly or unwittingly expressing it in our
behavior. Still, assumptions of moral relativity appear regularly in objections
to Christian faith. Budziszewski suggests countering a dishonest question
with a question, and he gives this example:

> A student once asked, "Isn't morality all just really relative? How do we even
> know that murder is wrong?" . . . I recognized at once that it was a smoke-
> screen. . . . So I responded, "Are you in any doubt about murder being
> wrong?" My student did not expect that reply. . . . Stumbling a bit he replied,
> "Some people might say that murder was right." I pressed. "Yes, but I'm not
> asking about some people. I'm asking about you. Have you any real doubt
> about murder being wrong for everybody?" Confronted in this way, he broke
> down and admitted, "No, I guess not." That gave me the opening to say,
> "Then tell me something that you are in doubt about." Now this was a mo-
> ment of truth for this student.[8]

A MOMENT OF TRUTH

Nothing in Christian witness is more important than to bring a person to
their own moment of truth. There are several ways that this occurs.

First, those you are speaking to may suddenly see what they have not
seen before and be led to place their faith in Jesus Christ. This is, of course,
the main goal of Christian witness among unbelievers.

Second, a person's moment of truth may be to recognize that they have
been playing with fire, that the issues that have kept them from following
Christ are nothing but a mask for self-justification. They may realize that
they need to become serious about their religious beliefs and behavior. Im-
plicitly they will know that "honesty is the best policy." Their moment of
truth requires that they start behaving in accord with what they know is
right. They then can move on in their spiritual quest with an open mind and
a willing heart.

Third, the moment of truth may *harden* their heart. The truth is there before the skeptics. They know that; they just refuse to follow their best judgment and wreak condemnation on themselves. As we have seen, the apostle Paul makes this clear in Romans 1:18-22. That can be a terrifying passage for a sinner to take seriously. When a central truth in the gospel is made plain, when it is understood by the listener and yet rejected, the moment of truth threatens an eternal consequence.

What would it take, we might ask, for Richard Dawkins, a self-confessed "fulfilled atheist," to change his mind about God or totally naturalistic evolution? Will any argument shake his confidence? Is his recalcitrance only a matter of his intellectual commitment to naturalism? Or is there something deeper? Is moral blindness also involved? Were he—the arch-advocate of neo-Darwinism—to change his mind about naturalistic evolution, would it not cost him his status among his scientist peers? If he were to come to faith in Christ, can we imagine the response of the academic community? Would it not take something more than a mere argument, even one based on scientific standards he accepts? Christian design scientists, for example, ask him only to consider the data arrived at by the methods of normal natural science while at the same time being open to an explanation that includes the notion of design. They are appealing to the argument of "best explanation"—that is, what best explains the phenomena everyone acknowledges are there.

When I have asked such questions of Christian colleagues who argue for the Christian faith in the context of academe, they tend to agree. As one of them put it, "It would take a personal crisis." When the roots of one's commitment reach deep into the heart, a change of theoretical mind includes a change in the heart nothing short of conversion. That sort of change does not come without something striking at the very roots of one's being. Does this mean that we should ignore the recalcitrant? Not at all. It only means that we should continue to do our best to make a good case for the Christian faith and pray that somehow, through whatever means, God will turn that good case into a *persuasive* one.

As Christian witnesses we can do nothing to force the acceptance of truth. How nonbelievers come to believe is their business and the business of the Holy Spirit. But we can, should and do pray that the moment of truth leads to Jesus as Lord and Savior.

PART THREE

GOOD ARGUMENTS
THAT WORK

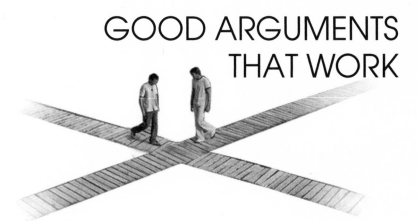

We have looked at arguments that should fail because they are flawed and at arguments that are good but often do not persuade. Now we turn to a more positive side and look at a couple of extended arguments that actually work.

First, however, we should note that the contexts of our witness vary a great deal. On the one hand are the many opportunities we get to talk about our faith to our friends and acquaintances. We have private dialogues across a table at Starbucks, casual conversations with fellow travelers on buses or planes, extended discussions with fellow members of neighborhood clubs, even chat rooms on the Internet. Here we begin wherever we can. If we are discussing anything but the weather, there will probably be an opportunity to raise issues that will take the conversation toward spiritual matters.

Second, there are often opportunities to speak of one's faith in public and semipublic forums. Christians on secular campuses, for example, automatically get involved in what we used to call "bull sessions" or, more quaintly, "squashes." These are excellent opportunities for students to hone their dialogical skills and learn what gets attention to the gospel, what falls flat, what offends, what works. Coffee breaks and lunchtimes at offices serve as openings for spiritual conversations as well. These, then, can be extended into private dialogues later.

Finally, some Christians are called to witness in public arenas. From the time I began teaching English composition as a graduate student, I have sought opportunities to present the case for the Christian faith in public forums. My early attempts fell quite flat, either because few turned up to my lectures sponsored by local InterVarsity Christian Fellowship groups or because if they did—well, who knows why! It was not until my book intended for Christians, *The Universe Next Door,* was published in 1976 that anyone seemed to pay attention to what I was saying. That book attracted more than Christian readers and has been instrumental in moving some people toward faith in Christ. From 1977 till the present, I have given hundreds of talks on the Christian faith. I have drawn from this experience in the preceding chapters.

In the chapters that follow we will look at two examples of effective public presentations of the gospel—one from the apostle Paul and one from my own ministry. From both of these I trust we will gain ideas and models that are transferable to any effective Christian witness—public or private, large group or individual. A Christian witness must never stop learning, either through practice or through study. The final chapter is an annotated bibliography to guide further study.

I SEE YOU ARE VERY RELIGIOUS

Paul in Athens

For a witness to the intellectual world, the seventeenth chapter of the book of Acts contains one of the most helpful accounts in the whole of the Bible. Here we see the incomparable apostle directly engaging the best non-Christian minds of his age. We don't have a detailed record of how they replied to him, but we can easily surmise much of it from Greek intellectual history. The whole encounter is instructive for our own both private and public witness.

PAUL'S TIME IN ATHENS

We begin with the setting itself. Paul had just encountered severe opposition in the previous two cities he had visited. In Thessalonica, the Jewish community rose up in arms when Paul talked about Jesus as the Messiah promised by Scripture and declared that he had risen from the dead. Jason, Paul's host, was attacked and dragged before the magistrates. So the other believers sent Paul and his sidekick Silas on down the coast to Beroea. There the Jews were more receptive, and both they and some elite Greek men and women believed. Nonetheless, Jews from Thessalonica followed Paul to Beroea, stirring up so much trouble that the believers took Paul away to Athens and returned with instructions to send along Paul's companions, Timothy and Silas, as soon as possible.

Athens was no longer in the prime of its glory. The days of Socrates, Plato and Aristotle were long gone. Still it was a major commercial city and—more important—the center of Greek philosophy. Paul's ministry in Athens repeated the pattern he had practiced many times before. He went to the synagogue to present Jesus as the Jewish Messiah and to the marketplace to engage ordinary Greeks in the hustle and bustle of conducting their ordinary business. There he got the attention not just of the general population but of the philosophers and orators as well. They asked him to give a more formal presentation to the council of the Areopagus of his case for what they took to be two new gods—Jesus and Anistasis ("the resurrection"). If their request followed a normal custom, Paul would have been given a day to prepare a speech that he would memorize and deliver. As Eckhard J. Schnabel says, it may be that "the speech Luke records in Acts 17:22-31 is the summary of a written source."[1] In any case, it is not merely a summary of Paul's usual teaching but a speech prepared for a specific audience, the learned elite of Athens.

The speech in Acts 17 is a master stroke of narrative and argument. Tightly organized, packed with detail and pregnant with implication, this passage bears close analysis. One way to expose its riches is to lay out its structure as we look at the content. The following text/outline can be read in two ways: first by reading only the regular text, ignoring the outline in italics; second, by reading the italics, which indicate the argumentative structure.

TEXT AND STRUCTURE: ACTS 17:16-34

Context of the argument

   16 While Paul was waiting for them in Athens, he was deeply distressed to see that the city was full of idols.

1. *Synagogue with Jews*

   17 So he argued in the synagogue with the Jews and the devout persons,

2. *Marketplace with general populace (Greeks)*

and also in the marketplace every day with those who happened to be there.

3. *Philosophers—Epicureans and Stoics*

[18] Also some Epicurean and Stoic philosophers debated with him.

Reaction of the philosophers

1. *Babbler*

Some said, "What does this babbler want to say?"

2. *Proclaimer of foreign divinities*

Others said, "He seems to be a proclaimer of foreign divinities." (This was because he was telling the good news about Jesus and the resurrection.)

New context—The "university"

[19] So they took him and brought him to the Areopagus and asked him, "May we know what this new teaching is that you are presenting? [20] It sounds rather strange to us, so we would like to know what it means." [21]Now all the Athenians and the foreigners living there would spend their time in nothing but telling or hearing something new.

The argument

1. *Point of contact—religious curiosity*

[22] Then Paul stood in front of the Areopagus and said, "Athenians, I see how extremely religious you are in every way. [23] For as I went through the city and looked carefully at the objects of your worship, I found among them an altar with the inscription, 'To an unknown god.'

2. *Solution to their curiosity*

What therefore you worship as unknown, this I proclaim to you.

    a. *The nature of the true God (unknown to them)*

²⁴The God who made the world and everything in it, he who is Lord of heaven and earth, does not live in shrines made by human hands, ²⁵ nor is he served by human hands, as though he needed anything, since he himself gives to all mortals life and breath and all things.

b. *The nature of human beings*

 (1) *Universality of created human nature*

  ²⁶From one ancestor he made all nations to inhabit the whole earth,

 (2) *Bounds of human history intended and set by God*

  and he allotted the times of their existence and the boundaries of the places where they would live,

 (3) *Purpose of human beings intended and set by God*

  ²⁷so that they would search for God and perhaps grope for him and find him—though indeed he is not far from each one of us.

 (4) *Intertwining relationship between God and human beings, as is already understood by the Greek poets*

  ²⁸For 'In him we live and move and have our being'; as even some of your own poets have said,
  'For we too are his offspring.'

c. *Implications of b(1) for the nature of God*

 ²⁹ Since we are God's offspring, we ought not to think that the deity is like gold, or silver, or stone, an image formed by the art and imagination of mortals.

d. *What God wants of human beings now—repentance in the light of judgment*

 ³⁰ While God has overlooked the times of human ignorance, now he commands all people everywhere to repent, ³¹because he has fixed a day on which he will have the world judged in righteousness

e. *The resurrected Jesus as warrant for belief in this unique God*
by a man whom he has appointed, and of this he has given assurance to all by raising him from the dead."

Response to the argument

[32]When they heard of the resurrection of the dead,

1. *Some scoffed.*

some scoffed;

2. *Some were willing to hear more.*

but others said, "We will hear you again about this."

3. *Some believed.*

[33]At that point Paul left them. [34]But some of them joined him and became believers, including Dionysius the Areopagite and a woman named Damaris, and others with them.

REASON AND RHETORIC

Paul's address to the Athenian philosophers is a masterful blend of reason and rhetoric. He had a message to give—a complex system of religious and philosophic thought that was in its essence foreign to his intelligent listeners. He knew his audience was both curious about the new ideas they were hearing and baffled by them.[2] Some thought he might just be another "babbler," literally "seed picker," a would-be philosopher out of his depth, a crazy foreigner who thought he could impress the intelligentsia. Moreover, they seem to have thought that Paul was promoting two gods—Jesus and Anistasis (The Resurrection). So Paul had his work laid out for him. How would he proceed? His reasoning would need to be wrapped in rhetoric.

On the one hand, he already had an audience. His comments in the marketplace had piqued lots of interest. On the other hand, this audience was potentially quite hostile (not that this ever stopped Paul!), both because of the pride associated with their being philosophers in the glorious city of

Greek philosophy and because of the commitments they had already made to views that ran counter to the gospel. Paul, however, had already done his homework, and he was ready to begin on common ground. So first he commended them for their interest in religious matters. The city god of Athens was, of course, Athena, but Greek religion had a host of deities of varying importance and stature. And while some of the philosophies were essentially atheistic, they all acknowledged one or more basic spiritual entities or principles. So Paul said, in effect, "I see that you don't want to miss acknowledging any of the gods. You honor lots of them and even have a statue to an unknown god." Then, having established common ground, he went on to explain the God they really didn't know, the one and only Creator-God of the Bible. Table 10.1 brings out the comparisons and contrasts.

What Paul said from here on makes clear that he understood not only that he was talking to philosophers but that these philosophers themselves were committed to different systems. The Epicureans, following their founder Epicurus (341-271 B.C.), thought that the goal of human existence was the "good life." They were not hedonists; they didn't seek the utter indulgence of their passions. Rather, they wanted the highest measure of happiness they could have in a world in which any happiness is hard to come by. So they cautioned against overindulgence even as they sought satisfaction of their desires. They were also naturalists; that is, they believed that matter is all there is in the world and that matter itself is composed of atoms, tiny particles of matter. Yes, there are celestial beings, gods, but they have no concern for people and can be safely ignored. Moreover, this life is all there is; there is no afterlife. As New Testament scholar E. M. Blaiklock puts their view, human beings should "limit wants, desires, and aspirations to this life only, be satisfied with simple pleasures, and insulate [themselves] from all disturbances of public life, and private passion or ambition."[3]

The Stoics, on the other hand, following Zeno (335-263 B.C.), emphasized the virtue of living in harmony with Reason (Logos), seen as the single unifying principle or mind of the universe. They placed major emphasis on human rationality and the value of individual self-sufficiency. Suicide is per-

Table 10.1. Comparison of Three Ancient Worldviews

Stoicism: Panentheism	Epicureanism: Practical Naturalism	Biblical Mind: Christian Theism
God is the Mind, Logos or principle of Reason that holds all reality together.	There is no God as such; there are celestial beings, but they have no concern for human beings.	God is the transcendent Creator and the Lord of creation (v. 24), not a local god.
God/universe is self-existent.	The gods/universe are self-existent.	God is self-existent (vv. 25, 29).
Human beings are an expression of God/universe.	Human beings are on their own.	Human beings are God's creation (v. 26).
Human beings are self-sufficient but should align themselves with Reason.	Human beings best live their lives by limiting their desires to simple pleasures.	Human nature is universal (v. 26).
The human longing for meaning is satisfied by living by Reason.	The good life involves insulating oneself from private or public ambition.	Human beings are designed to search out and find God (v. 27).
		People have a longing for God that can be fulfilled.
History is not a category of much interest.	History is not a category of much interest; one should avoid the disturbances of public life.	God is in charge of history—both events and their meaning. (vv. 26-27, 30-31)
God is immanent.		God is immanent (v. 28).
Human reason should align itself with the divine, that is, Reason itself.	The gods are not relevant to human life.	God is beyond any human imagination (v. 29).
There is no divine judgment.	There is no divine judgment.	God is judge (vv. 30-31) and holds us responsible for our actions.
There is no resurrection. Death is the end of each person's existence.	There is no resurrection. Death is the end of each person's existence.	[Jesus'] resurrection shows that God will judge us in him (v. 31).

mitted. After all, the Logos or World-Soul is impersonal and unconcerned with human fate. There is no afterlife.

It is worth noting that neither the Epicureans nor the Stoics had any substantial place for the plethora of gods whose statues peopled the parks and avenues of Athens. Yet both had adapted the spiritual aspect of their philosophies to the common customs of the city. Paul's "critique of idols (Acts 17:29) is a clear indictment of the popular piety with which the Stoic and Epicurean philosophers [had] accommodated their theoretical convictions to the religiosity of the populace so that people could continue to participate in the cultic activities of the cities."[4]

Paul, knowing these two basic philosophic commitments of his audience, wanted to make clear just what among these commitments he agreed with and what he opposed. Table 10.1 lays out the contrasts. Several of these need to be explained.

Perhaps the most interesting is Paul's use of lines from two Greek poets, the Stoics Artus of Soli and Cleanthes (vv. 28-29), whose work he uses to further bridge the gap between the Stoic and biblical concepts of fundamental reality. Taken in their own natural context, the first line ("in him we live and move and have our being") affirms the Stoic notion of the immanence of God (or God as Logos, the "mind of the universe" of which it is a part). The second line ("For we too are his offspring") links human beings (who are rational) with the Logos (Reason itself). Neither view is fully Christian, however, because for the Stoics, Reason was not so much a creator ex nihilo as the final substructure or emanator of all reality. Was Paul twisting poetry as the apostle Peter accused heretics of doing? Or was he pointing to the genuine (though somewhat distorted) insight of Stoic philosophy? In any case, he did not quote from any Epicurean text; this may suggest that they were the ones who scoffed while the Stoics were among those who wanted to hear more later.

Blaiklock explains it this way:

To win a basis of agreement Paul lays no emphasis on the personality of

God. *"We ought not to think,"* he says, *"that the divine nature (or 'deity' in the abstract) is like gold, or silver, or stone. . . ."* Stoicism was pantheistic *[I would say panentheistic]; the listening crowd was polytheistic. Paul begins with the simplest platform common to both: there is something divine, which the religious strive to please, and some philosophers to comprehend.*[5]

But in his closing remarks Paul did not avoid countering the Greek view (both Stoic and Epicurean) that God's existence makes no difference to human life and its aftermath. God is the judge of the living and the dead. Repentance is the only way toward the good life now and forever. Nor did he draw back from the key event that demonstrates God's concern both for the sins of human beings and for their salvation. Judgment is coming by the One who died and rose again, the one Son of God who incorporates the resurrection into himself, not as if The Resurrection were another god, but by rising from the dead. It was the resurrection, then, that clinched Paul's argument. The only God who is really God is the One who has come in human form, taught, died and rose again. He is both Judge and Savior.

It was indeed the resurrection that was the sticking point. The subtext in almost all ordinary Greek thought is the radical distinction between matter and spirit (Gnosticism), matter and form (Plato). No god could participate in matter and still be divine. A god might take human form, but only temporarily. But a god could never keep the material human form and remain fully divine or, for that matter, wholly good. Moreover, as Schnabel says, "The notion of life after death was foreign for both the Epicureans and the Stoics, who thought the 'art of dying' meant to teach people to accept their mortality."[6] Without a radical change of mind and heart at a fundamental level, a "Greek" could not become a follower of Jesus.

That indeed is the problem facing every Christian witness: the changing of the heart and mind is utterly out of an apologist's control. What is amazing, of course, is that people do change their minds. Though no church seems to have been formed in Athens, some became believers, one of whom was a woman and one a member of the Areopagus itself, a public forum, somewhat like a university, that was concerned with such matters as "foreign deities."[7]

A MODEL FOR TODAY

The account of Paul's time in Athens is pregnant with suggestions for a modern witness, especially one focused on the intellectual world. A list of these is easy to compile.

The social and intellectual contexts for apologetics

1. We can find a ready place to witness wherever we are—marketplace, workplace, home community.

2. We can expect to be misunderstood—there are few, even in so-called Christian America, who are able to discern the meaning of our God-words.

3. We should recognize the background assumptions of those we encounter—their materialism, New Age spirituality, commitment to Islam or Eastern thought, and mostly their fuzzy deism (the notion that while there is a God who made the universe he can mostly be ignored) or fuzzy theism (God is good to have around when one is in trouble).

4. We can take advantage of our open society. We glory in our freedom of speech. In Athens everyone, Greek or not, would "spend their time in nothing but telling or hearing something new" (v. 21). This sounds like conversations over coffee at Starbucks, or the content of radio and TV talk shows, or the lunchroom at the office. It is especially characteristic of our universities. In a culture that has lost its Christian character, genuine biblical understanding of Jesus Christ is utterly new!

The links between Christianity and culture

5. We can find the hooks that link the Christian message to the interests of our culture. People today are still "very religious"; most believe in some sort of God and pay intermittent lip service when trouble arises in their lives.

Of course, we need to correctly assess the context. Not all societies are religious—nor, as it turns out, committed to reason as an alternative. In the fall of 1991 I met Dan Clendenin, a philosopher who at that time was teaching Christian studies in the Department of Atheism at Moscow State University. He told me that religious consciousness among university students had been almost completely erased by Marxism. Clendenin saw very little of the spiritual hunger that supposedly characterized posttotalitarian Russia. Students were reading Lewis's *Mere Christianity,* but the arguments, he said, were running like water off their backs. It was okay, so it seemed, to be nonreligious in Russia, but not to be an atheist. To these students, atheism meant Communist Party ideology. On the other hand, few had an existential interest in religion. As one person was quoted as saying, "My parents really believed in communism, in socialism, in Lenin. We—well frankly, I would say we believe in nothing."[8]

Clendenin also observed a lot of historical skepticism. Some of his students did not think Jesus ever existed, and they were not even sure about Plato. They believed Napoleon did, however. Russians don't need to be totally logical, he said. Lewis's arguments seemed "too rational" for them. He thought that for them belief of a religious kind might very well come without rational justification.

Similarly, the apostle Paul knew his audience. They were interested in religious issues, and they held rationality in high regard. We should do our homework as well, following the example of both the apostle and Professor Clendenin. Those who wish to have an impact on teenagers and college students could well consult Smith and Denton's *Soul Searching: The Religious and Spiritual Lives of American Teenagers.*[9]

6. We can take great pains to explain the parts of the gospel that will appear "foreign"—for instance, the idea of God as both just and loving, the necessity of Jesus' sacrifice and the notion of grace.

7. On a popular level we can use illustrations from movies or TV shows, novels and poetry. Artus of Soli and Cleanthes will not be known, but J. R. R. Tolkien, C. S. Lewis, Mel Gibson and Mother Teresa usually will be.

On university campuses there is a wealth of material available to us. In every academic field there are ideas common to the Christian worldview. These can be used to show that Christianity is not completely out in left field intellectually. For example:

- Christians want to know the truth. We enjoy research and teaching.
- We respect the findings of science and engage in it ourselves.
- We believe all people can know, even the postmoderns.
- We believe that we can't know everything, nor can even the moderns.
- We recognize the value of human life and the environment.
- We value the human intellect.
- We reject blind faith.
- We are concerned for our own and our family's future.

The content of the gospel

8. We need to have a clear idea of the central teachings of the gospel. Paul included all of them: the nature of God as the sole transcendent and personal Creator; his control over the history of his creation; the universal nature of human beings as responsible to God and, though in a broken relationship with him, still designed to search and find God; the inevitable judgment of God; the mercy shown by God through the death and resurrection of Jesus; and the necessity for all people everywhere to repent.

Notice the order of these key notions as Paul presents them. Paul knows that he must emphasize God's judgment of sinful humanity, but he does not place it first. Paul began with matters that, even when they were a challenge to his audience, were more amenable to being understood. He left the tough sticking point till near the end. We may take our cue from that. Likewise, he mentions Jesus and his resurrection only after he has spoken of God's judgment, for Jesus cannot really be understood apart from the key role he plays as our Savior. Paul was quite unlike the proverbial campus open-air preachers who declaim judgmental passages from

Scripture and point to students as they walk by, calling them whores and whoremongers. Paul did not focus solely on the Athenians as sinners. And when he did so, he quickly pointed to the mercy of God in Jesus Christ.

The response to our argument

Paul's presentation of the faith did not, of course, produce only the results he desired. First, there was scoffing. There is no way to prevent people from laughing at the gospel and poking fun at the apologist, and we need to be ready for that. As I mentioned above, at the University of Texas when I gave a talk on Lewis Thomas, one Christian woman admitted that she was a creationist, at which point one of her professors exploded with ridicule. The personal cost of admitting that you believe anything outside the narrow box of naturalism can be heavy.

There will always be Richard Rortys to try to make the gospel look so silly that it is not even worth discussing.[10] Or Daniel Dennetts who would advise putting religions in cages when they violate his notion of what constitutes human dignity. Just as we shouldn't save the elephants from extinction if it means preserving nineteenth-century life in Africa, so, Dennett says, we shouldn't save the Baptists "if it means tolerating the misinforming of children about the natural world [creation science]."[11] Or the Richard Dawkinses who, as noted earlier, pen lines like these: "It is absolutely safe to say that if you meet somebody who claims not to believe in evolution, that person is ignorant, stupid, or insane (or wicked, but I'd rather not consider that)."[12]

Second, however, in Athens there was an openness to continue the dialogue. This should usually be taken as a positive sign. With our friends, our neighbors, our workmates, there will be other occasions to explain the gospel, when we can build on the groundwork laid earlier. Adults normally take a long time to change the course of their thinking enough to be genuinely converted.

Third, there will be some who do believe, and it will be time to help them grow in their faith through worship and education within the Christian community.

THE APOSTLE PAUL AT DESPERATE STATE UNIVERSITY

One way to see the relevance of Paul's address to the Athenian philosophers is to imagine what a twenty-first-century version might look like. Let's say such an apologist (call him Daniel) arrives on campus without really planning to do so. There he is in a dormitory lounge of Desperate State University, the intellectual capital of, say, Michigan. That's what one of my colleagues imagined when he wrote the following takeoff on Acts 17.

A Paraphrase for the University (Acts 17:22-31)

Men and women of the university, I see that in every way you are very religious. As I walked around the university, I observed carefully your objects of worship. I saw your altar called the stadium where many of you worship the sports deity. I saw the science building where many place their faith for the salvation of mankind. I found your altar to the fine arts where artistic expression and performance seem to reign supreme without subservience to any greater power. I walked through your residence halls and observed your sex goddess posters and beer can pyramids. Yet as I walked with some of you and saw the emptiness in your eyes and sensed the aching in your hearts, I perceived that in your heart is yet another altar, an altar to the unknown God who you suspect may be there. You have a sense that there is something more than these humanistic and self-indulgent gods. What you long for as something unknown, I want to declare to you now.

This God I am speaking of is your personal creator. He is not a fabrication or invention of mankind. He is not a part of creation; he stands above it. He is greater and more powerful than you have ever dreamed. This God has given you your life, and has set the boundaries of your life. The longing for eternity in your heart was placed there by him. You may try to grope for him, but he is already intimately involved in the creation. It is his creative work in you, his image, that makes it possible for you to engage in athletic activities, scientific endeavor, artistic expression, and even playfulness and sexual pleasure.

But this God is calling you to repent. You have worshiped your own creativity instead of acknowledging him as your creator. You have forgotten the giver of the gifts. You have rebelled against your creator and gone your own way of self-indulgence and self-worship. As a result you have perverted the gifts of life and creativity. You have abused your sexuality through careless indulgence. You have chosen the way of futility and death. God calls you to turn from serving these false gods to give you life to bring glory to the living and true God, your creator.

God has sent his son, Jesus Christ, into the world to save and judge the world. The man Jesus has come to set things right, to bring justice, to call us back as a warning before judgment. By his death he offers a way back to God, to save us from self-destruction. By his resurrection he has shown that he has come with power to save and judge the world. As a result, this Jesus has become the pivotal point in history, the central issue for us today, either the stepping stone or the stumbling block. He offers reconciliation with the creator and he alone can give it.*

This paraphrase is, of course, a somewhat expanded version of the text in Acts. No doubt Paul's speech was considerably longer than what we are given there. Like Paul, this speaker begins with something that his audience will recognize. Even secular students will recognize that the fervor they have for sports, the arts and pleasure has a religious cast. They will also recognize the ache in their heart, though not recognizing where it comes from.

It is interesting that Daniel is addressing undergraduates. He would not give quite the same speech to graduate students, faculty or administration. There he might well start with the quest for knowledge, academic recognition or power in university politics. But he would certainly note the empti-

---

*This paraphrase was written by Daniel Denk, staff member of InterVarsity Christian Fellowship, and used by permission. He has given this several times as a dorm talk, as have other IVCF staff.

Table 10.2. Comparison of Three Contemporary Worldviews

Academic Mind	Secular Student Mind	Biblical Mind
Naturalism	Fuzzy deism/theism	Theism
No god of any kind	Sports, arts, sex, pleasure	God is Creator, Lord of creation, the only God of All
The universe is self-existent or "just there."	The universe was perhaps made by God or a Force.	God is self-existent.
Human beings are a chance product of the impersonal plus time.	Human beings may be made by God but are mostly on their own.	Human beings are God's creation.
Each person is made either by society or a combination of nature, nurture and self-development.	Each person is unique and only responsible to themselves.	Human nature is cast in the image of God.
There is no God to search for, but much can be known about the universe.	God can mostly be ignored until one gets in trouble.	Human beings are designed to search for and find God.
People may long for meaning, but that will be satisfied only through human effort.	People can call out to God when trouble strikes.	People have a longing for God that can be fulfilled.
History is what people make it to be—both in event and meaning.	Not much thought given to where history is going.	God is in charge of history—both event and meaning.
	God may be immanent but is rarely perceived.	God is immanent.
God is the product of our imagination.	God is probably what each person imagines him, her or it to be.	God is beyond human imagination. He is who he is.
All moral judgment is made on the basis of human determination.	God is soft-hearted and forgiving, a cosmic grandfather.	God is judge.
There is no resurrection. Death is the end of each person's existence.	There is probably an afterlife of some kind, maybe heaven, maybe reincarnation.	Jesus' resurrection shows that God will judge us in Jesus Christ.

ness in the hearts of people here too. And the solution to their quest would be the same. God is in charge of the universe, thus in charge of what the research scientists are trying to understand and what the university should be attempting to accomplish. Jesus Christ as Logos is not only the Creator of the universe but the Lord of its meaning and the institutions that look for and disseminate it. And, of course, he is both Judge and Savior.

THREE WORLDVIEWS

The total intellectual context of Daniel's talk can be summarized by distinguishing between three basic worldviews (see table 10.2).

When Daniel gets to judgment and the resurrection, how will the students react? Won't he get the same response that Paul received? Some may head toward belief in Jesus, others may continue to be open, and some may scoff. Some, of course, would never listen in the first place, but then, all of Athens surely did not listen to Paul.

Dan Denk, the actual author of the paraphrase, tells me that when it is delivered, eyes light up; it gains the attention of students. As with my own speaking on campus, local Christians are the ones to do the follow-up, and the ultimate results are seldom known.

One thing we always know, most effective apologetics will need to combine reason and rhetoric in an imaginative way. There is always room for creativity in defending the faith. Dan's paraphrase has been one effective way to get the conversation going. One of my own attempts is described in the following chapter.

11

SO WHY SHOULD I BELIEVE ANYTHING?

Christian Witness in a Postmodern World

The apostle Paul knew that he was addressing an audience of Grecian intellectuals. He combined good reasons and effective rhetoric to fashion a credible witness that hit its target. We should attempt to do the same.

Today our audience is likely to be people who have a rather dim view of any proclamation of exclusive religious truth. If we say that Jesus is the only way to God, we are likely to be thought bigoted—just the sort of people no one should want to be. In chapter eight we have already considered how to respond to this challenge in a private setting. How can this approach be used in a setting more like the one Paul faced in Athens—that is, the public arena of a university? Here is a description of a lecture/discussion I have given over two hundred times in the past twenty-some years.

SOME BACKGROUND ASSUMPTIONS

Christians know some things that postmodern nonbelievers don't know: They know that God is the Logos, the all-knowing knower of all things. They know that human beings have been made in God's image. They know that people are therefore sometimes-knowing knowers of some things. The entire Bible assumes that people, despite their fallen condition, can know a great deal about God. Jesus assumed that his audience—whether his followers or his opponents—could reason. Once, for example, he gave the religious leaders five reasons that his contemporaries should know that he was the special one sent from God (see Jn 5:30-47).

The problem is not postmodern people's inability to reason. They reason all the time about both the ordinary (what shirt to wear to the banquet) to the highly significant (what man or woman to marry), from the material (what chemicals are in this sample) to the personal (what college is best for me). But there is a reticence to believe that reason can lead them to a religious "truth" that is any "truer" than its opposite. Traditional arguments for Christian faith, then, are dismissed before they can be considered. That is what must be changed. Their faith in reason must be restored.

RESTORING FAITH IN REASON

If people place more faith in their reason than they think they do, how can they come to see this? One answer to that question is to take them through a process of self-reflection. Here is how I have done this. But first a bit of history.

In the early 1980s, David Suryk, InterVarsity staff member for Illinois State University, asked me to give a lecture providing reasons for the Christian faith. I presented it under the title "Is Christianity Rational?" The question-and-answer period that followed was extended further as a dozen students gathered around a table in a college lounge. One, enamored with the objectivism of Ayn Rand, pushed the discussion on for another hour or so.

Several months later, I gave a similar talk under the same title at Rochester University. After the presentation, a student in the front row asked, "May I read something?"

Always leery of giving over the podium, I asked, "How long is it?"

"Two pages," he said.

That seemed reasonable. What he read turned out to be a response he had drafted to the publicized title, "Is Christianity Rational?" He laid out five reasons that it was not. I don't remember what any of them were, but I do remember that one was so weak as to be almost silly, one was quite sophisticated, and three were objections that had substance but that I thought I could handle well. I didn't want to make the student look silly by exposing the silliness of the silly objection, nor did I want to tackle the difficult one right off the bat, so I turned to one of the other three and answered that.

Then I said, "Before addressing any other of his five objections, does anyone else have a question?"

After a pause, someone in the back row said, "What about his second objection?" So I responded to that. And so it went. The first student's five objections provided the grist for the give-and-take for over an hour. Toward the end, the janitor was clicking the lights on and off to get us to leave so he could close the building for the night.

About six months later, I gave the same lecture at Harvard University. This time students plastered the square with posters posing the question "Is Christianity rational?" and several others, including "Why should anyone believe anything at all?" Immediately I recognized that this was the right question, and since then I have used it over a hundred times as the title. Oddly enough, I did not have to change my lecture one whit. It was already set up to answer the question.

But note this: "Is Christianity rational?" is a modern question; it assumes that rationality is good. "Why should anyone believer anything at all?" is a postmodern question. It probes behind rationality to discover what is most foundational.

THE STRUCTURE OF THE PRESENTATION

The sponsors' preparation for the lecture and the structure of my presentation are simple.

The sponsors' preparation. A week or so before the presentation, the sponsors of the lecture plaster the campus with posters emphasizing the title. On the day of the lecture (and sometimes the previous day as well), they conduct a survey using only the title question.[1] Students are given a small sheet of paper with the question on the top and asked to give their answer. Before the lecture I read the answers and choose from them the most insightful and most humorous to use as an introduction to the presentation. Here's an example of the former, from a Bryn Mawr student in 1989:

Basically it seems impossible to not believe in anything. Such an ad-venture would lead one spiraling into the complete uncertainty that Descartes experienced in his meditations. Even if one believes that one should not believe, that is, of course, something. It is the way the human mind works. Everyone needs a central reference point, and some sort of belief serves that.

Among the more flippant answers, this one stands out:

A little green monster I met in the restroom told me to believe.

In any survey and there have been many, this answer is almost always among them:

Why not?

Apparently a lot of students think this is uniquely clever! In any case, when I read a few of the answers, students are alternately amused and amazed. It's been a good way to get students to laugh—always a good thing to do at the beginning of a lecture that can get rather heavy as students begin to ask tough questions and make shrewd comments.

Section 1: Everybody "believes" something. After the warmup introduction, I briefly discuss the nature and necessity of belief. In the back of my mind is the idea—unstated in the lecture—that *to believe is to trust that one knows the truth.* The presentation is designed to demonstrate this without stating it.

I do, however, state that *everyone's knowledge rests on belief.* This is true in every human arena: in ordinary life (how can you be sure you are awake and not dreaming?), in science (how can you be sure the universe is orderly, that your vision when you read the instruments is accurate, that your mind is functioning properly?), in philosophy (how can you be sure that the law of noncontradiction actually applies to reality?), in religion (how do you know whether there is a God?). Strictly speaking, everyone's knowledge rests on pretheoretical commitments that cannot be proved, though it can be shown that some are more likely than others. The question is, therefore, what justifies the beliefs we do have? Should we have them?

Then, to illustrate the panoramic sweep of the issues that underlie an answer to the question why should we have them, I put a diagram on a chalkboard or overhead (see figure 11.1).

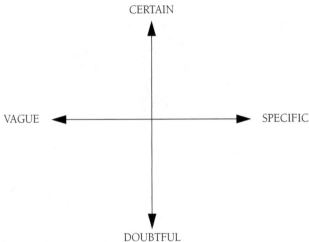

Figure 11.1

Some of our beliefs are psychologically quite certain; some are less so; some are doubtful indeed. Some of our beliefs (religious ones in particular) are specific and detailed: witness the lists of beliefs that are taught in the various catechisms and the strict religious traditions. Some are very vague (say, the notion that God is some sort of force). I explain what it is like the be in each of the quadrants: specific and certain, specific and doubtful, vague and certain, vague and doubtful. Then I further explain that we often move from one to the other. We begin, for example, believing what we are taught about God (or not God), and then after a few months at the university we wonder about these beliefs and eventually abandon them for doubt or substitute other beliefs in their place.

Then I ask three questions. The first two are thought questions:

1. Where are you on the chart?

2. Why are you where you are?

After a short pause for audience members to reflect (think!), I ask:

3. Why *do* people believe?

Their answers are then placed on the chalkboard (in four columns) as they are given. The columns are not labeled until students are asked where these "reasons" are studied in the university. What emerges quite easily from the students, then, are the categories: sociological, psychological, religious, philosophical. (These categories show how basic belief is, how many facets need to be explored before even its origins are understood.) Each column will have several entries, and others will be added in the discussion to follow. Table 11.1 shows the essential nature of what is received from student answers.

Table 11.1. Types of Beliefs

Sociological	Psychological	Religious	Philosophical
Parents	Comfort	Scripture	Consistency
Friends	Peace of mind	Pastor	Coherence
Society	Meaning	Priest	Completeness (best
Culture	Purpose	Guru	explanation of all
	Hope	Channeler	the above evidence)
	Identity	Church	

The next step is dialogic. Beginning with the sociological column, I ask students how good or strong these reasons are: "If, say, your parents were the only reason you had for believing what you do, would that be a good, strong reason or a weak one or no reason at all?" No student—well, almost none—will say parents are a good reason. So I ask why. The answers fall into two types. One ("It's not *my* belief") is psychological, so I add that to the psychology column. The other reason is more profound and helpful ("My parents might be wrong"), so I add "Right" or "True" to the philosophy column.

As the discussion proceeds through the other sociological reasons, it becomes clear to the students that none of the reasons is strong. Friends, society, even whole cultures could be significantly wrong about basic beliefs. So I point out that sociological factors—though they inevitably produce our original beliefs—are actually causes, a cause being something that makes you what you are, something that has had nothing to do with your own choice or consideration. In an era of I'm okay/you're okay, this realization does not go down well. Students want to be their own arbiters of belief.

As we proceed to examine each item in each column—sociological, psychological, religious—it becomes clear to the students that they themselves are using the category of truth to evaluate the strength of the reasons that are on the chalkboard. If a reason—say, "comfort"—is indeed a reason (which it is), is it a strong one? Only if giving comfort points to truth, and it does not always do that. Some things (like the drug thalidomide) give comfort in the short run and tragedy in the long run. A belief could give comfort until you died, but what then?

Scripture is a reason, but which Scripture—the Bible, the Qur'an, the Upanishads? They contradict each other. Contradictions can't all be true.

Eventually, the discussion is designed to produce in students themselves the recognition that they actually operate their lives based on whether they think something is true or not. A holy book, a pastor or guru, a religious tradition is worth trusting only if it points to the truth. So we end by briefly investigating tests for truth: consistency (logic), coherence, completeness (best explanation of all the evidence—public and private). The dialogue is now on the ground trod by traditional arguments.

Often only a very few philosophic reasons will have been suggested by students. The list of psychological and social reasons for belief will be long; the philosophical list will usually be quite short (though here it depends on who is attending—philosophy, engineering, psychology or arts majors).

In any case, at this point I hand out a bibliography (given at the end of this chapter) and offer five types of reasons that Christianity should be considered true. The lecture and this list are not so much a case for Christ as a

prologue to such a case. I do not develop the reasons but open the session
for questions after I have briefly explained each one:

1. Jesus himself is the best reason for believing in the truth of the Christian
   religion (a rationally strong, personally compelling reason).
2. The Gospels give a reliable account of what Jesus did and, especially, said
   about us and himself (rationally compelling).
3. The Christian worldview is consistent and coherent. It explains better
   than any alternative the vast array of phenomena presented to human beings (rationally strong, personally compelling).
4. Christians testify to their changed lives (philosophically weak but personally compelling).
5. The history of the church points to the attractiveness of Jesus' agenda, the
   kingdom of God; witness the St. Luke hospitals around the world (an am-
   biguous but ultimately positive reason).

I close the presentation with an encouragement to seek the truth: to read
the Gospels, to meet with Christian friends to study the Gospels with them,
and generally to hang out with those who know Jesus personally.

In the question-and-answer period I am open to questions of any kind,
hoping that more specifics of the gospel will be able to be presented. This
often happens. More important, groups who have sponsored this lecture/
discussion have usually followed up by encouraging those who have attended the lecture to join a small Bible study group where their questions
can be dealt with in depth over an extended period. It is in these groups and
further personal contact with the Christian community that commitments
to Christ are most likely to be made.

THE POSTMODERN CONNECTION

The appeal of this lecture/discussion to today's students is due in part, perhaps, to the connections it makes with postmodern students in a postmod-

ern culture. First, it does not assume that the best reason to believe is rationality; rather, it allows students to discover the value of rationality for themselves. Second, it stimulates self-reflection that leads to the recognition that it is, after all, the truth that one should believe. Third, it suggests how truth about spiritual matters can be acquired. Fourth, it provides a bridge from the personal and individual to the objective and communal. Fifth, it opens the door for the Bible to be heard as a legitimate source of truth. Sixth, it focuses attention on the reason above all other reasons for believing in the Christian faith: a personal encounter with Jesus Christ.

As time slips by and our university culture shifts and continues to lose its center, the approach of this lecture may no longer be effective. No matter. Even Harvard students can't be right forever. But Jesus can. He addresses every culture. May he direct us to those ways that help us make his presence known however and wherever our cultures—all of them—move!

BIBLIOGRAPHY

There are five basic reasons—or families of reasons—why anyone should believe Christianity is true. This bibliography provides a guide for anyone wishing to investigate these reasons. All five reasons are presented in James W. Sire, *Why Should Anyone Believe Anything at All?* (Downers Grove, Ill.: InterVarsity Press, 1994).

1. *The character of Jesus Christ as presented in the Gospels*

    The Gospels of Matthew, Mark, Luke and John in the Bible. See especially a modern translation such as the New International Version.

    Kreeft, Peter. *Between Heaven and Hell.* Downers Grove, Ill.: InterVarsity Press, 1982.

    Stott, John. *Basic Christianity.* 2nd ed. Downers Grove, Ill.: InterVarsity Press, 1971.

2. *The historical reliability of the Gospels*

    Barnett, Paul. *Is the New Testament Reliable?* 2nd ed. Downers Grove, Ill.: InterVarsity Press, 2005.

Blomberg, Craig. *The Historical Reliability of the Gospels.* Downers Grove,
Ill.: InterVarsity Press, 1987.

———. *The Historical Reliability of John's Gospel.* Downers Grove, Ill.: Inter-
Varsity Press, 2002.

Dunn, James D. G. *The Evidence for Jesus.* Philadelphia: Westminster, 1986.

Wenham, John. *Christ and the Bible.* 2nd. ed. Grand Rapids, Mich.: Baker,
1984.

3. *The internal consistency and coherence of the Christian worldview:* its power to
explain what we perceive in our surrounding environment, the wonders of
the cosmos, the greatness and wretchedness of human beings, the pervasive
quality of love, the notion of good and evil, the possibility of knowledge

Chesterton, G. K. *Orthodoxy.* Garden City, N.Y.: Image, 1959.

Lewis, C. S. *Mere Christianity.* New York: Macmillan, 1958.

Wenham, John. *The Enigma of Evil.* Grand Rapids, Mich.: Zondervan, 1985.

4. *The attractiveness of Christianity* in comparison to other religions and
worldviews

Neill, Stephen. *Christian Faith and Other Faiths.* Downers Grove, Ill.: InterVarsity Press, 1984.

Sire, James W. *The Universe Next Door.* 4th ed. Downers Grove, InterVarsity Press, 2004.

5. *The testimony of its adherents*

Colson, Charles. *Born Again.* Old Tappan, N.J.: Chosen, 1976.

Lewis, C. S. *Surprised by Joy.* New York: Harcourt Brace, 1966.

Goricheva, Tatiana. *Talking About God Is Dangerous.* New York: Crossroad,
1987.

6. *The witness of the church down through the ages*

Latourette, Kenneth Scott. *A History of the Expansion of Christianity.* Grand
Rapids, Mich.: Zondervan, 1970.

Shelley, Bruce. *Church History in Plain Language.* Waco, Tex.: Word, 1982.

12

FRAMING EFFECTIVE ARGUMENTS

A Guide to Literature

Have you read this far? Then you will need no urging to read more. And there is so very much more to read and to learn.

In this book I have focused on only one aspect of Christian witness: framing and expressing winsome arguments. Except as illustrations of rhetorical concerns, I have presented or evaluated only a few actual arguments. A vast sea of books and arguments lies before you. Navigating through it can be difficult. You won't become lost, but you may lose sight of the goal—glory to God through your presenting good arguments. It is easy to read from now till eternity and never get up and do what should be done.

So if you haven't done so already, before you read any more, set sail among your friends, workmates, relatives, whomever, and in your witness—casual and deliberate—note their responses. Then choose those books that will help you address their concerns. Before reading a second book in one area, read a significant book in each of several other areas. You will then have a more comprehensive grasp of the issues that trouble those who are skeptical or searching. You will also gain confidence that you can deal with these topics, some of which may be outside your own personal interest. Make it a point to become interested in a wider and wider set of concerns.

Here, then, are my recommendations. They are divided into ten categories. First are three sections on Jesus, the topic no Christian witness must ever ignore: (1) his character, (2) his resurrection and (3) the reliability of the Gospels. Next come (4) a list of general books on defending the faith (covering most issues in the field) and (5) a section on classic and creative works. Finally come books dealing with specific issues: (6) foundational commitments, alternative worldviews and religions, (7) the challenge of science and evolution, (8) the problem of pain, suffering and evil, (9) the existence of God, and (10) personal experience of God. Each category is introduced with general comments on the most valuable books. Full bibliographical data follow the commentary.

JESUS CHRIST: THE SINGLE BEST ARGUMENT FOR THE CHRISTIAN FAITH

The core reason for Christianity is the character of Jesus Christ. Those who speak for the faith should highlight Jesus, even at times to the exclusion of every other aspect. For when a seeker meets Jesus, the one who has argued for Christian faith can and should simply disappear. It sounds so easy, doesn't it? Just introduce your friends to Jesus; that's all you have to do. Yes, it is.

Now how do you do it? You do it by pointing to Jesus and then getting out of the way. So how do you point to Jesus? The best way is through getting the skeptic or young Christian to hear—by reading or listening to—the story of Jesus as told in the Gospels of Matthew, Mark, Luke and John. Any clear modern translation will do: New Revised Standard, New International Version or The Message, for example. Your job will be to highlight the value of reading these Gospels and to prompt the seeker to ask: Just who is the Jesus who emerges from the text?

In the final analysis the text of the Gospels is the authority, far more the authority than you or the books I list here. You and the books will take second place—perhaps an important second place, but second nonetheless. When a seeker meets Jesus, he or she has met the God with whom we all have to do, either now or later.

Is this mystical? Not really. You will simply be putting the seeker in the presence of Jesus. Then Jesus will speak through the text by the power of the Holy Spirit, who will be not so much a silent partner in the encounter as the hidden One who illuminates the Scripture, brings the seeker to *see* who Jesus is and prompts a proper response.

Other than to point to Jesus, your task will be to remove any obstacles to the seeker's seeing well. Many people will wonder whether they can trust the Gospels. They will raise questions about alleged contradictions. They will wonder whether they are being misled by biased translations or clever plots by a power-hungry clergy. It will help to respond well to these challenges. That's where the following books come in. Make it a life goal to read the Scriptures daily, learning all you can about Jesus from the authoritative texts and from books like the following. You will then have a wealth of perspective and detail to share as the skeptic turns to Jesus and then grows in Christ along with you. Defending the faith then continues, now confronting issues that involve both of you as believers and witnesses to God's grace.

The Character of Jesus Christ

Other than the Gospels, the first book I want in the hands of a seeker is John Stott's *Basic Christianity*. It clearly lays out the biblical case for who Jesus is and what he has done, and has been used worldwide in many translations in presenting the good news of Jesus. Three other excellent books on Jesus are *Understanding Jesus* by Alister McGrath and *The Challenge of Jesus* and *Who Is Jesus?* by N. T. Wright. The latter is Wright's popular distillation of his massive scholarly study *Jesus and the Victory of God*. Also going deeper than the first three books is Ben Witherington's *The Christology of Jesus*, a scholarly and technical study of Jesus' self-understanding.

Peter Kreeft, a clever modern defender of the faith, presents the liar-lunatic-Lord case for Jesus as God in *Between Heaven and Hell*. In *Socrates Meets Jesus* he imagines Socrates back from the dead, reading the Bible and becoming a believer in Christ. Through clever dialogues, these two volumes break down barriers modern skeptics often have to thinking that Jesus could be relevant to the twenty-first century.

On the most basic level, my own *Jesus the Reason* is an individual or group Bible study guide designed to introduce Jesus and to prompt an existential response to the dilemma of Jesus as liar, lunatic or Lord.

Highly Recommended

Kreeft, Peter. *Between Heaven and Hell: A Dialog Somewhere Beyond Death with John F. Kennedy, C. S. Lewis and Aldous Huxley.* Downers Grove, Ill.: InterVarsity Press, 1982.

―――. *Socrates Meets Jesus: History's Great Questioner Confronts the Claims of Christ.* Downers Grove, Ill.: InterVarsity Press, 1987.

McGrath, Alister. *Understanding Jesus.* Grand Rapids, Mich.: Zondervan, 1987.

Sire, James W. *Jesus the Reason: 8 Studies for Individuals or Groups.* 2nd ed. LifeGuides. Downers Grove, Ill.: InterVarsity Press, 2004.

Stott, John R. W. *Basic Christianity.* 2nd ed. Downers Grove, Ill: InterVarsity Press, 1970.

Witherington, Ben, III. *The Christology of Jesus.* Minneapolis: Fortress, 1990.

Wright, N. T. *Who Is Jesus?* Grand Rapids, Mich.: Eerdmans, 1992.

Recommended

Anderson, Norman. *Jesus Christ: The Witness of History.* Rev. ed. Downers Grove, Ill.: InterVarsity Press, 1985.

Wright, N. T. *The Challenge of Jesus: Rediscovering Who Jesus Was and Is.* Downers Grove, Ill.: InterVarsity Press, 1999.

Yancey, Philip. *The Jesus I Never Knew.* Grand Rapids, Mich.: Zondervan, 1995.

The Resurrection of Jesus

In the 1950s, when modernity was in full bloom, and even a decade or so later, arguments for the resurrection were a staple of the case for Christ. It was important that as many as possible of Christianity's odd notions be found reasonable. In fact, if the miraculous and the seemingly impossible could be proved, it lent great credibility to the Christian faith. Postmodernity has changed that. By the 1970s with the turn to the psychedelic and all its wonders, there was far less wonder in the resurrection. So Jesus was raised from the dead; well, Shirley Maclaine was a princess of the Elephants in prehistoric India. The amazing is no longer so amazing.

Moreover, religious notions are simply pieces of larger stories constructed by culture to explain the inexplicable. So long as they explain, they do not have to be objectively true. The historicity of the biblical narrative is beside the point. Those who argue for Christian faith on university campuses today do not spend much time on proofs that Jesus did in historical fact die and come back to life.

But the historicity of the gospel narrative cannot so easily be dismissed. Christianity is rooted deeply in history. If Jesus did not rise from the dead, then, as the apostle Paul said, all believers are most to be pitied, for nothing else about their faith is likely to be true either. There will have been no atonement. We will all die in our sins.

So the resurrection of Jesus in space and time is important. For that reason, the following books will be found helpful.

In recent years, little has been added to the case for the resurrection. John Stott's *Basic Christianity* sets it forth in a brief form that may be adequate for many. But more extensive treatments are found in *Did Jesus Rise from the Dead?* The latter contains a debate between two philosophers—Gary Habermas (Christian) and Antony Flew (atheist)—followed by rejoinders by other scholars. My own basic defense of the resurrection will be found in chapter 11 of *Why Should Anyone Believe Anything at All?*

Highly Recommended

Habermas, Gary, and Antony Flew. *Did Jesus Rise from the Dead?* Edited by Terry L. Miethe. San Francisco: Harper & Row, 1987.

Sire, James W. *Why Should Anyone Believe Anything at All?* Downers Grove, Ill.: InterVarsity Press, 1994.

Stott, John R. W. *Basic Christianity.* 2nd ed. Downers Grove, Ill.: InterVarsity Press, 1971.

The Historical Reliability of the Gospels

The main reason people give either for not reading or for paying scant attention to the Bible is that they do not trust it to be reliable. Even though most nonbelievers have actually read little or none of it, they are sure it is filled with errors and contradictions. They may think it's a book of wise instructions on how to live your life but believe as well that you can safely ignore it or disagree with it. After all, doesn't it condemn casual sex, divorce and homosexuality? We now know better.

But the truth of the Christian faith is tied to history: if certain events—such as the crucifixion and resurrection of Jesus, or the exodus of the Jews from Egypt—did not happen, the central core of Christianity is false. If the Gospel accounts of Jesus' life and teaching are not true, the liar-lunatic-Lord argument is ineffective. One has to eliminate legend from the mix. The primary evidence for these events is Scripture. So its historical reliability must either be assumed or be demonstrated to be very likely. That is what the books listed here succeed in showing.

One of the best and most basic places to begin is *Is the New Testament Reliable?* by Paul Barnett. More technical is *The Historical Reliability of the Gospels* by Craig Blomberg, who treats form criticism, redaction criticism, alleged contradictions and hermeneutic theory. Blomberg's *The Historical Reliability of John's Gospel* focuses on the Gospel most challenged for its historical trustworthiness. Likewise James D. G. Dunn in *The Evidence for Jesus* has an excellent introduction to the study of the differences among the Synoptic accounts of the same events and teachings; the question whether Jesus claimed to be God; the resurrection; and the early church from which the Gospels emerged. In *The Evidence for Jesus* R. T. France surveys both biblical and extrabiblical documents relating to Jesus.

Ranging more broadly, I. Howard Marshall in *I Believe in the Historical Jesus* gives a scholar's assessment of what can be known. And John Wenham in *Christ and the Bible* provides a classic defense of the reliability of both the Old and New Testaments, arguing that "belief in the Bible comes from faith in Christ, and not vice versa; and that it is possible to proceed from faith in

Christ to a doctrine of Scripture without sorting out problems of criticism" (p. 9).

Recently historical skepticism has been fueled by the Jesus Seminar, a small group of New Testament scholars who argue that very little can be known about Jesus. Though their radical conclusions are not shared by the majority of their academic peers, they have the ear of the popular media, and magazines such as *Time* and *Newsweek* publish accounts of their work at Christmas and Easter. Evangelical academics have responded with excellent critiques, one of the most accessible of which is *Jesus Under Fire*, a collection of essays edited by Michael J. Wilkins and J. P. Moreland.

At the forefront of evangelical New Testament scholarship is N. T. Wright, now bishop of Durham in England. The first three massive volumes of his five-volume series Christian Origins and the Question of God are required reading for those wishing to plumb the depths of the issues raised by Jesus Seminar scholars such as John Dominic Crossan. *The New Testament and the People of God* discusses the methodology of historical study of the Bible. *Jesus and the Victory of God* tackles head-on what can be known about Jesus' character, life and teachings. And *The Resurrection of the Son of God* deals in depth with the accounts of the resurrection.

Highly Recommended

Barnett, Paul. *Is the New Testament Reliable?* Downers Grove, Ill.: InterVarsity Press, 1986.

Blomberg, Craig. *The Historical Reliability of the Gospels.* Downers Grove, Ill.: InterVarsity Press, 1987.

———. *The Historical Reliability of John's Gospel.* Downers Grove, Ill.: InterVarsity Press, 2002.

Dunn, James D. G. *The Evidence for Jesus.* Philadelphia: Westminster Press, 1986.

Evans, C. Stephen. *The Historical Christ and the Jesus of Faith: The Incarnational Narrative as History.* New York: Oxford University Press, 1996.

France, R. T. *The Evidence for Jesus.* Downers Grove, Ill.: InterVarsity Press, 1986.

Marshall, I. Howard. *I Believe in the Historical Jesus.* Grand Rapids, Mich.: Eerdmans, 1977.

Wenham, John. *Christ and the Bible.* 2nd ed. Grand Rapids, Mich.: Baker Book House, 1984.

Wilkins, Michael J., and J. P. Moreland, eds. *Jesus Under Fire.* Grand Rapids, Mich.: Zondervan, 1995.

Wright, N. T. Christian Origins and the Question of God. 3 vols.: *Jesus and the Victory of God* (1996); *The New Testament and the People of God* (1992); *The Resurrection of the Son of God* (2003). All published Minneapolis: Fortress.

———. *The Contemporary Quest for Jesus.* Minneapolis: Fortress, 2002.

DEFENSE OF THE FAITH IN GENERAL

Two books that best carry forward the discussion begun in the present book are David K. Clark's *Dialogical Apologetics* and William Edgar's *Reasons of the Heart.* Clark is a professor of theology at Bethel Theological Seminary in St. Paul, Minnesota. Raised in Japan by missionary parents, he understands the difficulty of communicating across cultural and worldview differences. Clark gives an excellent survey of the major elements of proper defense of the faith and the various ways Christians have understood the task. His dialectical approach, sensitive as it is to rhetorical concerns, is consistent with my own, but it takes readers much deeper into just how effective arguments can be framed. *Dialogical Apologetics* is an excellent next book. So is *Reasons of the Heart,* again a book that treats both reason and rhetoric in a fashion similar to mine.

Because of my reticence to champion the often aggressive manner of some who argue for Christian faith, I highly recommend John Stackhouse Jr.'s *Humble Apologetics.* Stackhouse, a professor of theology and culture at Regent College in Vancouver, is specifically sensitive to both the contributions and the dangers of postmodern thought. His emphasis on humility is commendable. But he shows that humility does not mean weakness or that one must, so to speak, lose an argument to win a soul. Likewise, his "guide" for conversations about Christianity is filled with wisdom won from practice.

A fourth book high on my list of *required* reading for those who would defend the faith is *Handbook of Christian Apologetics* by Peter Kreeft and Ronald K. Tacelli. Both Kreeft and Tacelli are professors of philosophy at Boston College. They have assembled, as the subtitle says, "hundreds of answers to crucial questions" and have made access to these answers easy by the careful way they are organized and identified. Here are twenty arguments for the existence of God, five arguments for the divinity of Christ, five solutions to the problem of evil and so on; fifteen separate issues are addressed.

Biola University professor of philosophy and religion J. P. Moreland presents a similar excellent collection of arguments in *Scaling the Secular City*. This book is not for beginners, but it could well be a part of a maturing apologist's education. William Lane Craig's *Reasonable Faith* is a masterful and eminently clear presentation of the classical arguments for the Christian faith. His description of what constitutes an effective argument is especially helpful. At the highest academic end of intellectual apologetics is Moreland and Craig's *Philosophical Foundations for a Christian Worldview*. Also see *To Everyone an Answer: A Case for the Christian Worldview*, edited by Francis J. Beckwith, William Lane Craig and J. P. Moreland, a collection of essays on a wide variety of key issues by leading defenders of the Christian faith.

Christian apologetics has a long history. One of the best ways to get a sense of this is to read the texts L. Russ Bush has compiled in *Classical Readings in Christian Apologetics, A.D. 100-1800*. Not only are there major excerpts from Justin Martyr to William Paley, but Bush has added an excellent "bibliographical essay on apologetic writing in the nineteenth and twentieth centuries."

Highly Recommended

Beckwith, Francis J., William Lane Craig and J. P. Moreland, eds. *To Everyone an Answer: A Case for the Christian Worldview*. Downers Grove, Ill.: InterVarsity Press, 2004.

Bush, L. Russ. *Classical Readings in Christian Apologetics: A.D. 100-1800*. Grand Rapids, Mich.: Zondervan/Academie, 1983.

Clark, David K. *Dialogical Apologetics: A Person-Centered Approach to Chris-

tian Defense. Grand Rapids, Mich.: Baker Books, 1993.

Craig, William Lane. *Reasonable Faith: Christian Truth and Apologetics*. Rev. ed. Wheaton, Ill.: Crossway, 1994.

Edgar, William. *Reasons of the Heart: Recovering Christian Persuasion*. Grand Rapids, Mich.: Baker, 1996.

Kreeft, Peter, and Ronald K. Tacelli. *Handbook of Christian Apologetics: Hundreds of Answers to Crucial Questions*. Downers Grove, Ill: InterVarsity Press, 1994.

Moreland, J. P. *Scaling the Secular City: A Defense of Christianity*. Grand Rapids, Mich.: Baker, 1987.

Moreland, J. P., and William Lane Craig. *Philosophical Foundations for a Christian Worldview*. Downers Grove, Ill.: InterVarsity Press, 2003.

Stackhouse, John G., Jr. *Humble Apologetics: Defending the Faith Today*. New York: Oxford University Press, 2002.

Recommended

Allen, Diogenes. *Christian Belief in a Postmodern World*. Louisville, Ky.: Westminster John Knox, 1989.

Berger, Peter. *A Rumor of Angels: Modern Society and the Rediscovery of the Supernatural*. New York: Doubleday, 1969.

Clark, Kelly James. *Return to Reason: A Critique of Enlightenment Evidentialism and a Defense of Reason and Belief in God*. Grand Rapids, Mich.: Eerdmans, 1990.

Dyrness, William. *Christian Apologetics in a World Community*. Downers Grove, Ill.: InterVarsity Press, 1983.

Evans, C. Steven. *Pocket Dictionary of Apologetics and Philosophy of Religion*. Downers Grove, Ill.: InterVarsity Press, 2002.

———. *Why Believe? Reason and Mystery as Pointers to God*. Grand Rapids, Mich.: Eerdmans, 1996.

Knechtle, Cliffe. *Give Me an Answer That Satisfies My Heart and My Mind*. Downers Grove, Ill.: InterVarsity Press, 1986. Short answers to forty-one questions.

Kreeft, Peter, and Ronald K. Tacelli. *Pocket Handbook of Christian Apologetics*.

Downers Grove, Ill.: InterVarsity Press, 2003. Condensed from *Handbook* above.

Lewis, Gordon. *Testing Christianity's Truth Claims.* Lanham, Md.: University Press of America, 1990.

Little, Paul. *Know Why You Believe.* 5th ed. Colorado Springs, Colo.: Victor, 2003.

McGrath, Alister. *Intellectuals Don't Need God and Other Modern Myths: Building Bridges to Faith Through Apologetics.* Grand Rapids, Mich.: Zondervan, 1993.

Mitchell, Basil. *The Justification of Religious Belief.* New York: Oxford University Press, 1981.

Pinnock, Clark H. *Reason Enough: A Case for the Christian Faith.* Downers Grove, Ill.: InterVarsity Press, 1980.

Purtill, Richard L. *Reason to Believe.* Grand Rapids, Mich.: Eerdmans, 1974.

Sire, James W. *Why Should Anyone Believe Anything at All?* Downers Grove, Ill.: InterVarsity Press, 1994.

Sproul, R. C. *Defending Your Faith: An Introduction to Apologetics.* Wheaton, Ill.: Crossway, 2003.

Swinburne, Richard. *The Coherence of Theism.* Oxford: Clarendon, 1977. Highly technical.

CLASSIC AND CREATIVE WORKS

Many people become interested in the defense of Christian faith not because they are looking for answers to questions of faith but because they happened to read *Mere Christianity* or *The Screwtape Letters* by C. S. Lewis. Never before had they seen any one write and think so well about the Christian faith. Now they can't get enough of Lewis and his forebears, such as G. K. Chesterton (1874-1936) or Blaise Pascal (1623-1662), or the creative apologists, like Peter Kreeft, who have followed him.

Chesterton, for example, was a skeptical journalist before his conversion; after that he turned his clever wit to writing several influential defenses of Christianity, including *Orthodoxy* and *The Everlasting Man,* the latter of which influenced Lewis's early faith. Chesterton also wrote novels and short stories that embodied the Christian worldview in surprising ways. Father Brown, his mystery story detective, solved crimes by his peculiarly Christian insight into human nature. His stories and novels, like those of Fyodor Dostoyevsky, Flannery O'Connor, Walker Percy and Wendell Berry, embody a Christian vision of the world that makes an implicit case for the Christian faith.

Indeed, Christian literature over the past few centuries continues to attract a wide audience. When English literature students encounter the poetry of Geoffrey Chaucer, John Donne, John Milton, Gerard Manley Hopkins or T. S. Eliot, they do not have far to go to become interested in the faith that sustained them. Christian literature teachers can nudge students in that direction even in the heavily antireligious context of modern public schools. I did. Great Christian writers simply give the lie to the notion prevalent in academe that Christians are just a little lower than idiots in the intellectual food chain.

As a literary scholar, C. S. Lewis gives credence to the notion that Christians can think academically as well as anyone.[1] His Chronicles of Narnia are both clever stories that fascinate children and profound expressions of the struggle between good and evil in the cosmos. His science fiction works are both great reads for adults and astute critiques of naturalism and the danger of descent into the occult. They show that Christians need not limit their imagination to dryly realistic narrative.[2] His essays show the power of a Christian pen across a wide range of subjects. And finally his apologetic works—especially *Mere Christianity, The Problem of Pain* and *Miracles*—portray the workings of a deft mind and a compassionate heart. They are often listed by converts as key to their grasping the truth of Christian faith. Almost any title by Lewis continues to be a useful tool for apologists today.

Following the lead of Chesterton and Lewis, Peter Kreeft (mentioned above) has written several imaginative presentations of apologetic arguments. Evidencing much of the skill of Plato, Kreeft's witty dialogues demonstrate the analytic power of the Christian worldview and make credible cases for Christian faith. Chief among these is *Between Heaven and Hell*, a trialogue among C. S. Lewis (Christian), John F. Kennedy (naturalist) and Aldous Huxley (New Age pantheist). All three died on the same day (November 22, 1963), so Kreeft pictures them somewhere beyond death, their final fate not yet realized, talking about what they expect to happen and why. In *Socrates Meets Jesus,* my favorite of Kreeft's many books, Socrates wakes up in the basement of Broadner Library (read Widener Library) at Have It University (read Harvard), enrolled in the Divinity School. Socrates attends class, reads the Bible, becomes a believer, and in hilarious dialogues challenges his professor and fellow students with the truth of the Christian faith. In *The Best Things in Life* Socrates shows up on the campus of Desperate State University and raises questions about power, pleasure, truth and the good life. *The Journey* is also a dialogue: a seeker for truth finds himself in Plato's cave of illusion and gets help first from Socrates, then Moses and finally Lewis. In his pilgrimage the seeker moves from wondering whether he should wonder about the meaning of life to discovering God in Christ as the glorious end to his quest. *Yes or No?*—a dialogue between Sal the Seeker and Chris the Christian—takes up a dozen or so key issues that arise in apologetic discussions, for example, science and religion, the character of Jesus, the afterlife, the Bible as myth or history, and the nature of heaven and hell.

Putting any of these books in the hands of seekers can spark great conversations about issues of faith. They also make excellent choices for book discussion groups.

In literature arguing for the faith, perhaps the classic of classics is Blaise Pascal's *Pensées.* Best known in modern academic circles as philosopher, mathematician and physicist, Pascal had a dramatic and intense experience of God and toward the end of his life turned to reasons for Christian faith. *Pensées* is what its title suggests—a large and almost haphazard collection of "thoughts" about many issues. He is the Pascal of the much touted and much maligned "Pascal's wager," using mathematical reasoning to argue that if a one chooses Christian belief and it turns out to be true, one gains everything; if it turns out to be false, one loses nothing. My own fascination with Pascal, however, focuses on his several arguments that only Christian faith gives a satisfactory explanation of both the wretchedness and the glory of human nature. One can find in the *Pensées* the roots of many notions that appear in the work of Lewis, Chesterton, Francis Schaeffer and many other apologists. The *Pensées* is not for those unwilling to give lots of time to reading or thinking carefully in the wake it sets up in the mind. But it is well worth the effort. It should be on the must-read list of everyone who wishes to defend Christian faith today. Three modern books will help those new to Pascal: Douglas Groothuis's *On Pascal,* Thomas V. Morris's *Making Sense of It All: Pascal and the Meaning of Life* and Peter Kreeft's *Christianity for Modern Pagans: Pascal's "Pensées" Edited, Outlined and Explained.* The latter contains much of the text of the *Pensées.*

Finally, *C. S. Lewis and Francis Schaeffer,* Scott R. Burson and Jerry L. Walls's analysis of two of the twentieth century's most effective apologists, is especially valuable in showing the various ways the two dealt with similar themes. The final chapter, "21 Lessons for the 21st Century," distills the wisdom of their rhetoric as well as their reason and is, in the words of J. P. Moreland on the back cover, "worth the price of the book."

Highly Recommended

Burson, Scott R., and Jerry L. Walls. *C. S. Lewis and Francis Schaeffer: Lessons for a New Century from the Most Influential Apologists of Our Time.* Downers Grove, Ill.: InterVarsity Press, 1998.

Chesterton, G. K. *Orthodoxy.* 1908; many editions.

———. *The Everlasting Man.* 1925; reprint Garden City, N.Y.: Image, 1955.

———. *The Father Brown Stories.* London: Cassell, 1929. Collects five volumes of Father Brown mysteries.

Groothuis, Douglas. *On Pascal.* Belmont, Calif.: Thomas Learning/Wadsworth, 2003.

Kreeft, Peter. *The Best Things in Life: A Twentieth-Century Socrates Looks at Power, Pleasure, Truth and the Good Life.* Downers Grove, Ill.: InterVarsity Press, 1984.

———. *Between Heaven and Hell: A Dialog Somewhere Beyond Death with John*

F. Kennedy, C. S. Lewis and Aldous Huxley. Downers Grove, Ill.: InterVarsity Press, 1982.

———. Christianity for Modern Pagans: Pascal's "Pensées" Edited, Outlined and Explained. San Francisco: Ignatius, 1993.

———. The Journey: A Spiritual Roadmap for Modern Pilgrims. Downers Grove, Ill.: InterVarsity Press, 1996.

———. Socrates Meets Jesus: History's Great Questioner Confronts the Claims of Christ. Downers Grove, Ill.: InterVarsity Press, 1987.

———. Yes or No? Straight Answers to Tough Questions About Christianity. Ann Arbor, Mich.: Servant, 1984.

Lewis, C. S. The Chronicles of Narnia. 7 vols.: The Lion, the Witch and the Wardrobe (1950); Prince Caspian (1951); The Voyage of the "Dawn Treader" (1952); The Silver Chair (1953); The Horse and His Boy (1954); The Magician's Nephew (1955): The Last Battle (1956); all published in New York by Macmillan.

———. Mere Christianity. New York: Macmillan, 1952.

———. Miracles: A Preliminary Study. New York: Macmillan, 1947.

———. The Problem of Pain. New York: Macmillan, 1940.

———. The Screwtape Letters. New York: Macmillan, 1942.

———. The Space Trilogy. 3 vols.: Out of the Silent Planet (1938); Perelandra (1943); That Hideous Strength (1945); all published in New York by Macmillan.

Morris, Thomas V. Making Sense of It All: Pascal and the Meaning of Life. Grand Rapids, Mich.: Eerdmans, 1992.

Pascal, Blaise. Pensées. Trans. A. J. Krailsheimer. Harmondsworth, U.K.: Penguin, 1966.

FOUNDATIONAL COMMITMENTS, ALTERNATIVE WORLDVIEWS AND RELIGIONS

As I emphasized in chapter six, a major reason for the failure of good arguments to persuade is the fundamental commitment people have made to false or problematic ideas and values. This factor has been a major focus of my own ministry of contending for the faith and has resulted in *The Universe Next Door,* a catalog of basic worldviews—theism, deism, naturalism, nihilism, existentialism, Eastern pantheistic monism, the New Age and postmodernism. I believe that it is vital for apologists to have a basic grasp of these fundamental orientations in order, first, to understand where they themselves stand and, second, to identify where their conversation partners are coming from. *The Universe Next Door* also analyzes worldviews and shows the superior strength of the Christian worldview. I would like to see its approach to audience analysis become second nature to Christian witnesses. It is the pattern of witness that has undergirded most of my own Christian witness.

Here is its general form: First, a Christian witness becomes intimately familiar with his or her own Christian worldview, attempting as much as possible to understand every aspect. Second, the witness recognizes that, whether they know it or not, everyone—Christian or not, young or old, Western or Eastern—has a worldview. Third, the witness knows (for good reason) that every non-Christian worldview is predicated on (1) the autonomy of human reason or (2) commitments to false gods or (3) highly dubious foundational presuppositions. Fourth, the Christian believes that if he or she can discern what these presuppositions are, it can be shown that, when taken to their logical conclusion, these presuppositions (1) will contradict one another, (2) can be shown to be so speculative or counter to obvious evidence that their credibility is greatly weakened or (3) are not the presuppositions that actually undergird the person's actions. (Combinations of any or all of the above are possible.) Schaeffer called this taking the roof off the non-Christian's house. Fifth, when those holding the inadequate worldview discover its inadequacy, the Christian can introduce them to the Christian worldview at precisely the point or points at which the non-Christian's worldview has revealed its weakness.[3]

Until recently the major challenge to Christian faith has come from the naturalists—those who tout the virtues of no faith whatsoever. In a section below, I will recommend books arguing for the existence of God. Here are Christian challenges to naturalism itself. Chief among these for the lucidity of their arguments are Lewis's *Miracles* and *The Abolition of Man*. Armand Nicholi, a Christian psychologist at Harvard University, has made a stellar presentation of the contrasting lives and views of C. S. Lewis and Sigmund Freud in *The Question of God*, also well produced as a television documentary.

Mature apologists also have a grasp of alternative religious commitments. Among the host of good books are Winfried Corduan's *Neighboring Faiths* and Norman Anderson's *Christianity and World Religions*. Both clearly delineate the basic beliefs of other major world religions and show the uniqueness of Christianity, giving the lie to the popular notion that all religions boil down to the same thing. With the growing impact of Islam around the world, Islam must be singled out for special attention. Here Colin Chapman's *Cross and Crescent* and Chawkat Moucarry's *The Prophet and the Messiah* are valuable resources. For stellar analysis and rejection of religious relativism, one can do little better than Harold A. Netland's *Dissonant Voices* and *Encountering Religious Pluralism*.

For postmodern twists in worldview, I suggest Douglas Groothuis's *Truth Decay* and Nancy Pearcey's *Total Truth*. The former lays bare the incoherence of postmodern understandings of "truth." The latter is Francis Schaeffer in overdrive—simply the best piece of cultural analysis in recent decades. It will do more to help a Christian to grasp Western culture at the beginning of the twenty-first century than a high stack of books by other critics, including me.

For in-depth analysis of individual alternate worldviews and religions, I suggest these: David K. Clark and Norman L. Geisler, *Apologetics in the New Age: A Christian Critique of Pantheism;* Douglas Groothuis, *Unmasking the New Age;* and James Herrick, *The Making of the New Spirituality.*

Highly Recommended

Anderson, Norman. *Christianity and World Religions.* 2nd ed. Downers Grove, Ill.: InterVarsity Press, 1984.

Chapman, Colin. *Cross and Crescent: Responding to the Challenge of Islam.* Downers Grove, Ill.: InterVarsity Press, 2003.

Corduan, Winfried. *Neighboring Faiths: A Christian Introduction to World Reli-

gions. Downers Grove, Ill.: InterVarsity Press, 1998.

Groothuis, Douglas. *Unmasking the New Age*. Downers Grove, Ill.: InterVarsity Press, 1986.

———. *Truth Decay: Defending Christianity Against the Challenges of Postmodernism*. Downers Grove, Ill.: InterVarsity Press, 2000.

Herrick, James A. *The Making of the New Spirituality: The Eclipse of the Western Religious Tradition*. Downers Grove, Ill.: InterVarsity Press, 2003.

Lewis, C. S. *The Abolition of Man*. New York: Macmillan, 1947.

———. *Miracles: A Preliminary Study*. Macmillan, 1947.

Moucarry, Chawkat. *The Prophet and the Messiah: An Arab Christian's Perspective on Islam and Christianity*. Downers Grove, Ill.: InterVarsity Press, 2001.

Netland, Harold. *Dissonant Voices: Religious Pluralism and the Question of Truth*. Grand Rapids, Mich.: Eerdmans, 1991.

———. *Encountering Religious Pluralism: The Challenge to Christian Faith and Mission*. Downers Grove, Ill.: InterVarsity Press, 2001.

Pearcey, Nancy. *Total Truth: Liberating Christianity from Its Cultural Captivity*. Wheaton, Ill.: Crossway, 2004.

Sire, James W. *The Universe Next Door*. 4th ed. Downers Grove, Ill.: InterVarsity Press, 2004.

Recommended

Brown, Colin. *Miracles and the Critical Mind*. Grand Rapids, Mich.: Eerdmans, 1984.

Clendenin, Daniel B. *Many Gods, Many Lords: Christianity Encounters World Religions*. Grand Rapids, Mich.: Baker, 1995.

Geivett, R. Douglas, and Gary R. Habermas, eds. *In Defense of Miracles: A Comprehensive Case for God's Action in History*. Downers Grove, Ill.: InterVarsity Press, 1997.

Groothuis, Douglas. *Confronting the New Age: How to Resist a Growing Religious Movement*. Downers Grove, Ill.: InterVarsity Press, 1988.

Swinburne, Richard. *The Concept of Miracle*. London: Macmillan, 1995.

THE CHALLENGE OF SCIENCE AND EVOLUTION

I argued in chapter seven that the issue of evolution is so emotionally charged that, unless it is introduced by a skeptic, it should be avoided. Well, the topic will come up, and it cannot be avoided. So those who speak for the Christian worldview should be prepared. In fact, they should be prepared for two quite different situations, first with skeptics, then with Christians. With skeptics, the issue—amazingly—is relatively simple. Here the goal should not so much be to refute biological evolution as a theory as to help the skeptic see that the real issue is not *how* the biosphere came to be in its present state but whether God was involved. That issue cannot be resolved solely within the framework of evolutionary theory. It involves philosophic and/or theological assumptions. There is, however, a value in showing that current evolutionary theory, based as it is on totally naturalist premises, does not explain all that it claims to explain; that, contrary to Richard Dawkins, it does not allow one to be an "intellectually fulfilled atheist." This then opens the way for the skeptic to consider the case for the existence of God, especially a case focusing on Jesus.

The second situation arises in conversations with Christians whose faith the apologist is trying to provide with foundations. The fact is that there is no consensus among informed and intelligent Christians. So every apologist needs to have an informed position, either one of the several specific options Christian experts have outlined and promoted or a position like my own—that no position is obviously correct and that it is not necessary to decide which one is correct. The key issue is not *how* God did it but *whether* he did it. The details can be safely left to those with the interest and ability to sort it out.

Evolution is, of course, only one issue in the broader context of science. It will be vital, therefore, to have a good grasp of the relationship between science and the Christian faith. For this I recommend one book most highly: *The Soul of Science: Christian Faith and Natural Philosophy* by Nancy R. Pearcey and Charles B. Thaxton. It surveys the history of the relationship and sets the stage for understanding the challenge of Darwinian evolution. A second helpful book, by philosopher of science Del Ratzsch, is *Science and Its Limits*. Finally, John Polkinghorne's *The Way the World Is* comes recommended by a chemist friend.

When we turn from science in general to evolution in particular there is one issue on which I do have a specific view—the nature of the Genesis account of origins. Henri Blocher's *In the Beginning* has convinced me that the first chapters of Genesis do not address the issue of creation from the standpoint of science but rather embody in a literary form the theological notion of creation ex nihilo by a personal God, a view of the cosmos and humankind's place in it that radically differs from the various ancient pagan creation mythologies. On the one hand, this frees the Genesis accounts from any charge of bad science. On the other hand, it means that no modern scientific cosmogony will find much in Genesis of any direct "scientific" use. Genesis is simply not addressing scientific matters. Of course, it does address metaphysical issues, and these interface with science on a fundamental level.

Christian scholars and scientists, as I mentioned above, take a variety of views of evolution and whether it squares with Christian faith. In *Science and Christianity: Four Views,* edited by Richard F. Carlson, each of the four scholars presents his own specific solution. These range from *creationism,* the notion that an inerrant Scripture is the authority on everything it touches including scientific issues; *independence,* the idea that the Bible deals with theological and moral issues but does not touch science and that science has nothing to do with religion; *qualified agreement,* which includes the views of the design scientists; and *partnership,* which holds that there is an interface between the Bible and science, a view that comports with what I have called *theistic evolution* in chapter five. Perhaps the most important values of this collection is, first, to show how Christians with quite different views of science and faith can discuss the issues without raising their voices and, second, to alert the beginning apologist to the complexity of the issues. This volume should strike humility in the heart of every Christian apologist whose training in science is limited.

The number of books on evolution has skyrocketed in the past two decades, not the least reason being the publication in 1986 of *Evolution: A Theory in Crisis* by Michael Denton. While not written by a Christian, it raised questions that are still largely unanswered by Darwinian evolutionary theorists. In the same year came militant atheist Richard Dawkins's *The Blind Watchmaker*, a clarion call against anything other than a universe that has evolved without a design or a designer. These books triggered responses from Phillip E. Johnson, a Christian law professor with a specialty in argumentation: *Darwin on Trial* in 1991 and then a series of follow-up publications that contest the case for evolution. When biologist Michael Behe's *Darwin's Black Box* was published in 1996, the argument took a critical turn. There was now reason to believe that evolutionary theory would never be able to explain the origin of many "irreducibly complex" biological mechanisms. It will be important for apologists to be fully aware of these developments.

Other key books relating to "design science" are *The Design Revolution* by William Dembski, *Icons of Evolution* by Jonathan Wells, *Signs of Intelligence* edited by William Dembski and James Kushiner, and *The Privileged Planet* by Guillermo Gonzalez and J. W. Richards. The story of the progress of the argument for "design science" is told by Thomas Woodward in *Doubts About Darwin: A History of Intelligent Design*. Theistic evolutionists, however, are still in the majority among Christians who are practicing scientists. See Keith B. Miller's collection of papers, *Perspectives on an Evolving Creation*.

Two videos, *Unlocking the Mystery of Life* (intelligent design in the biosphere) and *The Privileged Planet* (intelligent design in the cosmos) make excellent introductions to the relation of Christian faith to science (available at <www.illustramedia.com>).

The literature on evolution seems to grow exponentially. The Christian journal *Perspectives on Science and Christian Faith*, published by the American Scientific Affiliation (65 Market Street, Ipswich, MA 01938), keeps tabs on this through book reviews, articles and notes.

Highly Recommended

Behe, Michael, *Darwin's Black Box*. New York: Free Press, 1996.

Blocher, Henri. *In the Beginning: The Opening Chapters of Genesis*. Downers Grove, Ill.: InterVarsity Press, 1984.

Carlson, Richard F., ed. *Science and Christianity: Four Views*. Downers Grove, Ill.: InterVarsity Press, 2000.

Dawkins, Richard. *The Blind Watchmaker*. New York: W. W. Norton, 1986.

Dembski, William. *The Design Revolution: Answering the Toughest Questions About Intelligent Design*. Downers Grove, Ill.: InterVarsity Press, 2004.

Dembski, William A., and James M. Kushiner, eds. *Signs of Intelligence: Understanding Intelligent Design*. Grand Rapids, Mich.: Brazos, 2001.

Denton, Michael. *Evolution: A Theory in Crisis*. Bethesda, Md.: Adler and Adler, 1986.

Gonzalez, Guillermo, and Jay W. Richards. *The Privileged Planet*. Washington, D.C.: Regnery, 2004.

Johnson, Phillip E. *Darwin on Trial*. 2nd ed. Downers Grove, Ill.: InterVarsity Press, 1993.

————. *Reason in the Balance: The Case Against Naturalism in Science, Law and Education*. Downers Grove, Ill.: InterVarsity Press, 1995.

Miller, Keith B., ed. *Perspectives on an Evolving Creation*. Grand Rapids, Mich.: Eerdmans, 2003.

Pearcey, Nancy R. and Charles B. Thaxton. *The Soul of Science: Christian Faith and National Philosophy*. Wheaton, Ill.: Crossway, 1994.

Polkinghorne, John. *The Way the World Is*. Grand Rapids, Mich.: Eerdmans, 1983.

Ratzsch, Del. *Science and Its Limits: The Natural Sciences in Christian Perspective*. 2nd ed. Downers Grove, Ill.: InterVarsity Press, 2000.

Wells, Jonathan. *Icons of Evolution: Science or Myth?* Washington, D.C.: Regnery, 2000.

Woodward, Thomas. *Doubts About Darwin: A History of Intelligent Design*. Grand Rapids, Mich.: Baker, 2003.

THE PROBLEM OF PAIN, SUFFERING AND EVIL

The presence of pain, suffering and evil in light of a God who is all good, all knowing and all powerful leads to perhaps the most potent and most frequent objection to Christian faith. Fortunately a host of Christian theologians, Bible scholars, philosophers and apologists have addressed the issue. Unfortunately, none of the various responses has emerged as a knock-down solution. Still, a few major ways to deal with the problem have a great deal to recommend them, and one can find them in many of the books already listed in the "general" category above, notably those by Kreeft and Moreland, Kreeft and Tacelli, Knechtle, Dyrness and Little. My own brief treatment of the problem will be found in *Why Should Anyone Believe Anything at All?*

For deeper and more extended analyses, I have found the following titles most helpful. Henri Blocher in *Evil and the Cross* explains the major ways the problem has been addressed and concludes that the only satisfactory response is in the cross of Christ. If the problem is to be "solved," I too believe that it will be done only by those who so deeply rest their soul in Christ that they see the problem of evil from a divine dimension. Blocher's book is a rich mine of thoughts and insights to be contemplated at length. I am likewise impressed with John Wenham's profound treatment of the goodness of God in *The Enigma of Evil;* he treats the issue in both biblical and modern times. *How Long, O Lord?* by D. A. Carson plumbs the problem, especially as it confronts Christians who already trust that God is somehow both good and all powerful and yet allows great suffering and despicable evil. The Old Testament's attitude to war is seen by many skeptics as a special stumbling block. Peter C. Craigie addresses that well in *The Problem of War in the Old Testament.*

There would be no justification—ever—for not mentioning a pair of books that by their very existence highlight two major aspects of the problem of pain, the intellectual and the personal. In *The Problem of Pain* (1940) C. S. Lewis addresses the intellectual problem: how can a good God allow so much evil? And he provides a clever and clear analysis of the issue, seeming to lay to rest any trouble he might himself have had with it. After the death of Joy Davidman, whom he married late in life, Lewis was attacked by such grief that it led to deep doubt. This he describes in *A Grief Observed* (1961), the first edition of which was published under a pseudonym. No longer jaunty in tone, as was *The Problem of Pain*, this book plumbs deeply into the psychospirituality of a brilliant Christian whose faith is being severely tested. Read back to back, the two books come very close to squaring a circle.

Finally, for a heavy-duty philosophic defense of the goodness of God, there is *God, Freedom and Evil* by Alvin Plantinga. This book is not for the faint of mind, but for the intellectually gifted Christian and the full-blown philosophic skeptic, the case it makes is impressive.

Highly Recommended

Blocher, Henri. *Evil and the Cross.* Trans. David G. Preston. Downers Grove, Ill.: InterVarsity Press, 1994.

Carson, D. A. *How Long, O Lord? Reflections on Suffering and Evil.* Grand Rapids, Mich.: Baker, 1990.

Craigie, Peter C. *The Problem of War in the Old Testament.* Grand Rapids, Mich.: Eerdmans, 1978.

Kreeft, Peter. *Making Sense out of Suffering.* Ann Arbor, Mich.: Servant, 1986.

Lewis, C. S. *A Grief Observed.* 1961; reprint San Francisco: HarperSanFrancisco, 1994.

———. *The Problem of Pain.* New York: Macmillan, 1962.

Plantinga, Alvin. *God, Freedom and Evil.* Grand Rapids, Mich.: Eerdmans, 1974.

Wenham, John. *The Enigma of Evil: Can We Believe in the Goodness of God?* Grand Rapids, Mich.: Zondervan, 1985.

DOUBT

The dark shadow of doubt falls across the whole spectrum of issues and arguments in defense of Christian faith.

"Yes," the skeptic says, "I see the reasons to believe in the resurrection. Yes, I understand why the problem of evil does not have to defeat the case for God as both all good and all loving. Yes, it is clear that the theory of evolution does not explain what it claims to explain. The idea of intelligent creation is far more intellectually satisfying. But I am not convinced. I am nagged by doubt—doubt on both sides of these issues. What if, I keep thinking—what if it's all a pipe dream, the wishful thinking of the overly optimistic?"

Christian believers, too, are often plagued by doubt. They have believed, they have trusted, but they are sorely pressed by questions that won't go away. In the case of both the skeptic and the believer, various versions of the problem of pain and suffering and evil often sparks it. It is often helpful for each doubter to see that they are not alone, that reflection on doubt is as old as humankind. "Did God say . . . ?" the Tempter asked. And many a psalmist has puzzled over just how long God will take to comfort the afflicted.

Today we are fortunate to have a host of Christian apologists who have dealt with doubt in both profound and creative ways. Five titles top of my list of helpful books. The first is Lesslie Newbigin's *Proper Confidence*. Newbigin, a long time scholar and missionary in India, shows why the quest for philosophic certitude has led to nihilism and presents a case for "proper confidence" as an alternative. While I do not accept his view of Scripture, his understanding of what we can expect to know as fallen human beings redeemed and bent on knowing and serving God largely undergirds the approach I have taken in the present book.

In *God in the Dark* Os Guinness identifies a variety of causes for doubt and for each outlines a way for the doubter to respond. In *When Faith Is Not Enough* Kelly James Clark is especially empathic as he describes the character of doubt and its effects. But he goes much further. Via expositions of Ernst Becker's concept of the self and Søren Kierkegaard's three stages of life, Clark illuminates the joy of an authentic life of faith. A fourth title, introduced above, is also highly relevant: C. S. Lewis's *A Grief Observed* displays the existential anguish of a man who in losing his wife turns in despair to doubt the goodness of God.

Finally, I want to single out the book that helped me during graduate school as I struggled not so much with intellectual doubt as with the nagging sense that perhaps what I had committed myself to so many years before really couldn't be justified by rational thought. I didn't think my faith was false so much as that I could not find sufficient reasons for thinking it true. Bernard Ramm's *The Witness of the Spirit* calmed my mind and went a long way toward satisfying my soul.

Highly Recommended

Clark, Kelly James. *When Faith Is Not Enough.* Grand Rapids, Mich.: Eerdmans, 1997.

Guinness, Os. *God in the Dark: The Assurance of Faith Beyond a Shadow of a Doubt.* Wheaton, Ill.: Crossway, 1966.

Lewis, C. S. *A Grief Observed.* London: Faber and Faber, 1961.

Newbigin, Lesslie. *Proper Confidence: Faith, Doubt and Certainty in Christian Discipleship.* Grand Rapids, Mich.: Eerdmans, 1995.

Ramm, Bernard. *The Witness of the Spirit.* Grand Rapids, Mich.: Eerdmans, 1960.

Recommended

Bavinck, Herman. *The Certainty of Faith.* St. Catherines, Ont.: Paideia, 1980.

Clouser, Roy. *Knowing with the Heart: Religious Experience and Belief in God.* Downers Grove, Ill.: InterVarsity Press, 1999.

Dubay, Thomas. *Faith and Certitude.* San Francisco: Ignatius, 1985.

THE EXISTENCE OF GOD

Arguments for the existence of God are both ancient and often repeated. Some apologists already mentioned—especially Kreeft and Tacelli, and Moreland and Craig—present and analyze them. Moreover, they also appear in elaborate form in several works that deserve to be highlighted.

As I have noted in earlier chapters, I am not impressed by most of these arguments. The first and most important reason is that I think that John Calvin was basically correct in thinking that human beings are endowed with an immediate apprehension of the existence of God. He called this the *sensus divinitatus*. This sense is not something one can precisely identify, the way one can identify the eye as source of one's sight or the ear as the source of one's hearing. Rather, the sense of God's existence is simply an immediate apprehension like the sense that one is awake: something we take for granted until there is some doubt, such as when we suspect that we are dreaming. For an elaboration of this concept, see Roy Clouser's *Knowing with the Heart*.

But there are other reasons for my distrust in arguments for God's existence. Some arguments are so technical that they can be understood only by the highly intelligent. Some either fail for some flaw or flaws in the argument itself or yield such a thin concept of God that they move the skeptic no more than an inch toward the Christian concept of God that yet remains a mile away. Still, the maturing apologist should be aware of the arguments; occasions may well arise when they will prove useful.

Single volumes of special worth include *The Existence of God* by Richard Swinburne, *He Who Is* by E. L. Mascal, *God and Philosophy* by Étienne Gilson, *God and Other Minds* by Alvin Plantinga, and, more recently, *God, Reason and Theistic Proofs* by Stephen T. Davis.

Somewhat more accessible is the collection of papers edited by Christian philosopher J. P. Moreland and atheist philosopher Kai Nielsen. The collection is prefaced by a very helpful essay explaining why the existence of God is really worth debating (despite, I might add, those like myself who still wonder). Then *Does God Exist?* presents the case both pro and con, each author analyzing and rebutting the other's arguments. Then others, both Christian (William Lane Craig, Dallas Willard and Peter Kreeft) and non-Christian (Antony Flew and Keith Parsons), weigh in. Interestingly, the book is published by Prometheus Books, which specializes in promoting atheism and secular humanism.

Highly Recommended

Clouser, Roy. *Knowing with the Heart.* Downers Grove, Ill.: InterVarsity Press, 1999.

Davis. Stephen T. *God, Reason and Theistic Proofs.* Grand Rapids, Mich.: Eerdmans, 1997.

Gilson, Étienne. *God and Philosophy.* New Haven, Conn.: Yale University Press, 1941.

Mascal, E. L. *He Who Is: A Study in Traditional Theism.* London: Darton, Longman and Todd, 1966.

Moreland, J. P., and Kai Nielsen. *Does God Exist? The Debate Between Theists and Atheists.* Buffalo, N.Y.: Prometheus, 1993.

Plantinga, Alvin. *God and Other Minds.* Ithaca, N.Y.: Cornell University Press, 1967.

Swinburne, Richard. *The Existence of God.* Oxford: Clarendon Press, 1979.

THE PERSONAL EXPERIENCE OF GOD

I rather imagine that the most prevalent practical argument for the Christian faith is the story Christians tell about their own conversion. The argument is, of course, rationally weak. After all, everyone has some sort of story about his or her encounter with the divine. Why should I believe yours? Rhetorically, however, conversion stories carry lots of weight and sometimes make people we talk with suddenly perk up and take notice of what is at stake.

In this category we have God's own plenty from which to choose. I will mention only a few that I think are especially helpful for Christians to recall during conversations with seekers. The first is C. S. Lewis's *Surprised by Joy,* the account of his very gradual adult conversion from atheism to full-blooded Christian faith. Another, perhaps more relevant a decade or so ago than now, is *Born Again* by Watergate conspirator Charles Colson. He explains how Lewis's *Mere Christianity* played a role in his coming to faith. Colson's *The Good Life* details the experiences of many others who have found such life in Christ. Among the most dramatic and striking accounts, however, is Tatiana Goricheva's *Talking About God Is Dangerous.* Russian dissident

Goricheva takes us behind the scenes in the philosophy graduate-student world of Moscow State University before the fall of communism, recounting her move from Marxist-Leninism through existentialism and yoga to Orthodox Christian faith. From a long-term Christian with a less troubled personal life comes John Stott's *Why I Am a Christian*. Then, too, there is a book that sparked a flurry of interest among intellectuals when I lectured in Podgrica, Montenegro: *Albert Camus and the Minister* by Howard Mumma.

For apologists involved with the academic world, three collections are especially helpful. Kelly James Clark brings together the conversion stories of eleven philosophy professors in *Philosophers Who Believe,* and Thomas V. Morris adds twenty more in *God and the Philosophers*. In a third volume, *Professors Who Believe,* Paul M. Anderson draws together accounts from across the entire academic spectrum. These volumes make fascinating reading, brilliantly illustrating one of the major theses of the present book: Christ may be the only way to God, but there are many ways to Christ.

Highly Recommended

Anderson, Paul. M., ed. *Professors Who Believe: The Spiritual Journeys of Christian Faculty.* Downers Grove, Ill.: InterVarsity Press, 1998.

Clark, Kelly James, ed. *Philosophers Who Believe: The Spiritual Journeys of Eleven Leading Thinkers.* Downers Grove, Ill.: InterVarsity Press, 1993.

Colson, Charles. *Born Again.* Old Tappan, N.J.: Chosen Books, 1976.

Colson, Charles, with Harold Fickett. *The Good Life.* Wheaton: Tyndale House, 2005.

Downing, David. *The Most Reluctant Convert: C. S. Lewis's Journey to Faith.* Downers Grove, Ill.: InterVarsity Press, 2002.

Goricheva, Tatiana. *Talking About God Is Dangerous.* Trans. John Bowden. New York: Crossroad, 1987.

Lewis, C. S. *Surprised by Joy: The Shape of My Early Life.* London: Geoffrey Bles, 1955.

Morris, Thomas V., ed. *God and the Philosophers: The Reconciliation of Faith and Reason.* New York: Oxford University Press, 1994.

Mumma, Howard. *Albert Camus and the Minister.* Brewster, Mass.: Paraclete, 2000.

Stott, John R. W. *Why I Am a Christian.* Downers Grove, Ill.: InterVarsity Press, 2004.

FINAL WORDS FROM AN ANCIENT PREACHER AND A MODERN WAG

The writer of Ecclesiastes (12:12) was at least half right:

Of making many books there is no end, and much study is a weariness of the flesh.

I like the first half. Still, the T-shirt given me on my retirement from InterVarsity Press may say it best:

So many books, so little time.

NOTES

Preface

[1]William Lane Craig recounts this in *Reasonable Faith: Christian Truth and Apologetics*, rev. ed. (Wheaton, Ill.: Crossway, 1994), p. 74.

I Believe—Help My Unbelief

[1]Alfred Lord Tennyson, "In Memoriam A. H. H.," poem 54. A. H. H. is Arthur Henry Hallam, Tennyson's close friend, who died at age twenty-two.

[2]I have tried to explain and justify this definition of "humble apologetics" in *A Little Primer on Humble Apologetics* (Downers Grove, Ill.: InterVarsity Press, 2006). Just before putting the finishing touches on this book, I read a quotation from theologian John Oman that struck me as a parallel to my definition of apologetics: "There is only one right way of asking men to believe, which is to put before them what they ought to believe because it is true; and there is only one right way of persuading, which is to present what is true in such a way that nothing will prevent it from being seen except the desire to abide in darkness; and there is only one further way of helping them, which is to point out what they are cherishing that is opposed to faith. When all this has been done, it is still necessary to recognise that faith is God's gift, not our handiwork, of His manifestation of the truth of life, not of our demonstration by argument or of our impressing by eloquence" (*Grace and Personality* [New York: Association Press, 1961], p. 121, as quoted by Martin E. Marty, *Varities of Unbelief* [Garden City, N.Y.: Anchor Books, 1966], pp. 198-99).

Chapter 2: You're All Hypocrites!

[1]Luke is especially clear about his attempt to set straight the story of Jesus (Lk 1:1-4). On some occasions the Gospel authors have included information that would

not have been expected by either the writer or the audience. For example, unless it actually was women who first learned of Jesus' resurrection, this detail would surely not have been included in the Gospel accounts, for at the time women were not considered credible witnesses in court. The story of the resurrection gains credibility by such unusual details.

[2]Alfred North Whitehead, *Science and the Modern World* (1925; reprint New York: Mentor, 1948), p. 25.

[3]Quoted by Greg Jesson, "Beyond Ideological Impasses: Francis Schaeffer on Truth, Community and the Life of Discussion," *Witherspoon Fellowship Lectures,* no. 37 (November 17, 2004), p. 11.

Chapter 3: It's Dangerous to Believe You're Right

[1]Immanuel Kant thought he could understand the foundation of cause, but his philosophy is notorious for its difficulty. See Roger Scruton, *Kant,* Past Masters (Oxford: Oxford University Press, 1982), pp. 22-40, for a clear exposition of this facet of Kant's thought.

[2]Jerry Falwell as quoted by Andrew Sullivan, "This Is a Religious War," *New York Times Magazine,* October 7, 2001, available at <www.query.nytimes.com/search/restricted/article?res=FA0814FF39590C748CDDA90994D9404482>.

[3]Sullivan, "This Is a Religious War."

[4]Ibid.

[5]Ibid.

[6]Ibid.

[7]Thomas L. Friedman, "Foreign Affairs; The Real War," *New York Times,* November 27, 2001, available at <www.query.nytimes.com/search/restricted/article?res=F30810F73A5E0C748EDDA80994D9404482>.

[8]David Schnaider, letter to the editor, *New York Times,* November 29, 2001, sec. A, p. 34.

[9]See Christian Smith and Melinda Lundquist Denton's excellent sociological analysis of why teenagers from a variety of different Christian denominations and other religions have adopted Moralistic Therapeutic Deism as a background belief system (worldview): *Searching: The Religious and Spiritual Lives of American Teenagers* (New York: Oxford University Press, 2005), pp. 172-92.

[10]Sigmund Freud's version of wish fulfillment is, of course, much more sophisticated than the popular versions. In *The Future of an Illusion* he argues that the notions of the gods and religion arose from the attempt of our primitive ancestors to explain and deal with a hostile natural and human environment. "The gods retain their threefold task," Freud says. "They must exorcise the terrors of nature, they must reconcile men to the cruelty of Fate, particularly as it is shown in death, and they

must compensate them for the sufferings and privations which a civilized life in common has imposed upon them" (trans. W. D. Rodman-Scott, rev. by James Strachey [Garden City, N.Y.: Anchor, 1964], p. 24). In other words, belief in God fulfills the *wish* for this threefold task to be accomplished. And any belief is "an illusion when a wish fulfillment is a prominent factor in its motivation, and in doing so we disregard its relation to reality, just as the illusion itself sets no store by verification" (ibid., p. 49). Freud argues that unlike religious notions, his own explanation is based on science. It is ironic that precisely this so-called scientific foundation has been called in question; Freud's own explanation has largely been rejected by the scientific community. That has not, however, kept the "popular" versions from remaining popular. For a brief but telling critique of Freud, see William Edgar, *Reasons of the Heart: Recovering Christian Persuasion* (Grand Rapids, Mich.: Baker, 1996), pp. 79-84. Also see William Dyrness, *Christian Apologetics in a World Community* (Downers Grove, Ill.: InterVarsity Press, 1983), pp. 133-40; and Armand M. Nicholi Jr., *The Question of God: C. S. Lewis and Sigmund Freud Debate God, Love, Sex and the Meaning of Life* (New York: Free Press, 2002).

[11]Augustine *Confessions* 1.1.

[12]John Calvin *Institutes of the Christian Religion* 1.3.1.

[13]As Scott Burson and Jerry L. Walls point out, C. S. Lewis called this Bulverism: "the notion that your opponent's thoughts are tainted but yours are not." See their *C. S. Lewis and Francis Schaeffer: Lessons for a New Century from the Most Influential Apologists of Our Time* (Downers Grove: InterVarsity Press, 1998), p. 161; and C. S. Lewis, "Bulversim," in *God in the Dock: Essays on Theology and Ethics,* ed. Walter Hooper (Grand Rapids, Mich.: Eerdmans, 1970), p. 273.

[14]Edward Sisson, "Darwin or Lose," *Touchstone,* July/August 2004, p. 40. Moreover, attributing nonrational motives to someone is a subtle form of *argument ad hominem,* discussed in the following chapter.

[15]Friedrich Nietzsche, "On Truth and Lie in an Extra-moral Sense," in *The Portable Nietzsche,* trans. Walter Kaufmann (New York: Viking, 1954), p. 46.

[16]Michel Foucault, "Truth and Power" (from *Power/Knowledge*), in *The Foucault Reader,* ed. Paul Rabinow (New York: Pantheon, 1984), p. 74.

[17]Richard Rorty, "Relativism: Finding and Making," in *Philosophy and Social Hope* (London: Penguin, 1999), p. xxvi.

Chapter 4: You Have Insulted Us All

[1]I learned later that Richard Dawkins gave the same response when Phillip Johnson asked him about Michael Behe's *Darwin's Black Box.* See Thomas Woodward, *Doubts About Darwin: A History of Intelligent Design* (Grand Rapids, Mich.: Baker, 2003), p. 162.

[2]Philosopher David Beck has put me on to at least one previous use of a similar story in John Locke's *Essay Concerning Human Understanding.* Locke identified it as originating in India. His use of the story is so different from mine that any response to it by subsequent critics would be irrelevant.

Part 2: Good Arguments That Often Fail

[1]Note that *validity* is an assessment of the form of an argument, not the truthfulness of its conclusion. An argument can be valid in form even if its premises are false, but then its conclusion is likely to be false as well. Logic and the fallacies of deductive reasoning are explained in more detail in J. P. Moreland and William Lane Craig, *Philosophical Foundations for a Christian Worldview* (Downers Grove, Ill.: InterVarsity Press, 2003), pp. 28-66.

[2]William Lane Craig, *Reasonable Faith: Christian Truth and Apologetics,* rev. ed. (Wheaton, Ill.: Crossway, 1994), p. 41.

[3]Ibid., p. 50.

[4]Ibid.

Chapter 5: People Can't Communicate. What?

[1]George Mavrodes, "There Was a Wind Blowing," in Thomas V. Morris, *God and the Philosophers: The Reconciliation of Faith and Reason* (New York: Oxford University Press, 1994), pp. 212-13.

[2]By *rhetoric* I mean the "art of persuasion" or "the art of framing and presenting effective arguments." Or, as Aristotle said, "Rhetoric may be defined as the faculty of observing in any given case the available means of persuasion. . . . [It is] the power of observing the means of persuasion on almost any subject presented to us" (*Rhetoric* 1.2 in *The Basic Works of Aristotle,* trans. Richard McKeon [New York: Random House, 1941], p. 1329). This art, of course, can be corrupted by employing means of persuasion—such as emotional appeal (anger, sentiment, vilification of those who disagree) that lend nothing to the likelihood of the truth of one's argument. But effective *rhetoric* as such is a component in most successful presentations of the truth.

[3]John G. Stackhouse Jr., *Humble Apologetics: Defending the Faith Today* (New York: Oxford University Press, 2002), p. xvi.

[4]Ibid., p. 72.

[5]At Urbana 93, InterVarsity's triennial missionary conversion, I watched seventeen thousand people sit in rapt attention as Ravi Zacharias presented a rational argument for the Christian faith. Yes, he told a few stories. Yes, he is dynamic as a speaker. Yes, he has charisma. But no, he did not "entertain." No, he did not major in massive, mindless, manipulative maneuvers. No, he did not even engage in the

kinds of rhetorical ploys I am using in this alliteration and these parallel sentences (or, if he did, I didn't notice). Rather he presented an *argument.* Afterward, three hundred cassettes of his talk sold in a few hours. Some five hundred more were made, and they too sold.

[6]Bill Watterson, from *Calvin and Hobbes* (1995), reproduced in *Insight* (newsletter of Institute for Advanced Studies in Culture, Center on Religion and Democracy at the University of Virginia), Fall 2004, p. 5.

[7]Since there are so many Christians who delight in debate, it was a pleasure for me to find that Stackhouse too finds debate a poor vehicle for the gospel. He calls them "power encounters between champions," and he asks, "How can any medium of power convey the gospel of grace?" Then he notes, "Dorothy L. Sayers once quipped, 'Controversy is bad for the spirit, however enlivening to the wits,' but public religious debate seems to be deadly for both soul and mind" (Stackhouse, *Humble Apologetics,* pp. 220-21, quoting Barbara Reynolds, *Dorothy L. Sayers: Her Life and Soul* [New York: St. Martin's/Griffith, 1993], p. 82).

[8]Stackhouse describes one apologist during a question-and-answer period: "He condescended to friendly Christian questioners, cutting them off to re-pose their questions in a way he thought improved them. And any critical questioner was met with a palpable impatience and a long-winded reply, with no opportunity for a rejoinder. It was, in my view, a disgraceful example of a speaker egocentrically out of touch with his audience" (*Humble Apologetics,* p. 144).

Chapter 6: I Don't Get It

[1]Alvin Plantinga says, "It is difficult to find much by way of noncircular argument or evidence for the existence of God" ("A Christian Life Partly Lived," in *Philosophers Who Believe: The Spiritual Longings of Eleven Leading Thinkers,* ed. Kelly James Clark [Downers Grove, Ill.: InterVarsity Press, 1993], p. 69).

[2]True, the argument in a very basic form does not require twenty-four pages; Peter Kreeft and Ronald K. Tacelli do so in fewer than three pages. To defend the argument with any rigor, however, even twenty-four pages are minimal. See Peter Kreeft and Ronald K. Tacelli, *Handbook of Christian Apologetics: Hundreds of Answers to Crucial Questions* (Downers Grove, Ill.: InterVarsity Press, 1994), pp. 58-60.

[3]J. P. Moreland, *Scaling the Secular City* (Grand Rapids, Mich.: Baker, 1987), p. 42.

[4]The reservations I am expressing about the value of rational arguments are much like those expressed by Pascal. Douglas Groothuis identifies these as follows: "1. Metaphysical proofs for God's existence are remote from reasoning in that they are involved or complex. 2. What is remote from reasoning has 'little impact' existentially because of its complexity and tentativeness; one would be afraid of making a mistake in reasoning. 3. Therefore, metaphysical proofs have little existential im-

pact. 4. True knowledge of God (that is, religiously relevant understanding) cannot be remote from reason and have little existential impact (implied). 5. Therefore, metaphysical proofs cannot deliver any true knowledge of God" ("Are Theistic Arguments Religiously Useless? A Pascalian Objection Examined," *Trinity Journal,* 1994, p. 151). I agree with the first three of these but am loath to accept the fourth and fifth.

My concern is not so much with the validity or soundness of abstract arguments but with whether they are likely to convince any but a very few skeptics. See the remarks made by George Mavrodes, which I quote in chapter five (p. 73). Only five of twenty Christian philosophers who recount how they came to believe in Christ mention reason as a major factor: see Kelly James Clark, ed., *Philosophers Who Believe: The Spiritual Journeys of Eleven Leading Thinkers* (Downers Grove, Ill.: InterVarsity Press, 1993), and Thomas V. Morris, ed., *God and the Philosophers: The Reconciliation of Faith and Reason* (New York: Oxford University Press, 1994). One of these, C. Stephen Evans, even says that "few (if any) come to faith primarily because of evidence or arguments" (in Morris, *God and the Philosophers,* p. 92).

Christians who are seeking further justification for what they already believe may, of course, be helped a great deal. In any case, Christians who disagree with Pascal's and my reservations about the value of rational argument may take courage from Groothuis's analysis: he examines each of Pascal's five reservations and rejects them all.

[5]R. Douglas Geivett, "Is Jesus the Only Way?" in *Jesus Under Fire,* ed. Michael Wilkins and J. P. Moreland (Grand Rapids, Mich.: Zondervan, 1995), pp. 189-200. See also Geivett's later discussion of the kalam argument in *To Everyone an Answer: A Case for the Christian Worldview* (Downers Grove, Ill.: InterVarsity Press, 2004), pp. 61-76. The history of this argument will be found in William Lane Craig, *The Kalam Cosmological Argument* (London: Macmillan, 1979), pp. 1-60.

[6]Richard Swinburne, *The Existence of God* (Oxford: Oxford University Press, 1979).

[7]Christians attracted to abstract arguments often are—or think they are—quite intelligent. Their skill in abstract thought tempts them to overconfidence and arrogance. One need not yield to temptation, of course, but believing one has an especially strong case for some detail of Christian belief makes it easy to look down on those who either cannot follow the argument or, when they do, remain unconvinced.

[8]John Wilson "Intoxicated with Tomatoes," *Books and Culture,* May/June 2004, p. 5. Wilson cites Eire's *Waiting for Snow in Havana* as reviewed by Miroslav Volf in *Books and Culture,* January/February 2004. Wilson goes on to quote from "Ode to the Tomato," a ecstatic poem by Pablo Neruda, commenting that it is not the tomato itself that is a proof of God's existence but "the tomato as seen by the poet Pablo Neruda,

a maker made in the Maker's image, and as received by us, 'sub-creators' too" (ibid.). This argument is reminiscent of Kreeft and Tacelli's aesthetic argument for the existence of God: "There is the music of Johann Sebastian Bach. Therefore there must be a God. You either see this or you don't" (Kreeft and Tacelli, *Handbook of Christian Apologetics*, p. 81).

[9]Madeleine L'Engle would seem to agree. Kelly Monroe quotes her: "On the far side of complexity we are found not by an argument, but, as Madeleine L'Engle said at a California Veritas Forum, 'a light so lovely that those who see it will be drawn to its presence.' And in that light all things become clear" (Kelly Monroe, from the prologue to a forthcoming book).

[10]Paul Chamberlain points out in a personal communication that if the person with whom the Christian is speaking is a convinced atheist, then an argument for theism may well have "the potential to establish the framework with in which a message about Jesus (God revealed in human form) makes sense."

[11]Christian Smith and Melinda Lundquist Denton quote and summarize the views of teenagers about who God is: "In short, God is something like a combination Divine Butler and Cosmic Therapist: he is always on call, takes care of any problems that arise, professionally helps his people to feel better about themselves, and does not become too personally involved in the process" (*Soul Searching: The Religious and Spiritual Lives of American Teenagers* [New York: Oxford University Press, 2005], p. 165).

[12]These questions come from simple surveys conducted at these institutions just before I gave my lecture "Why Should Anyone Believe Anything at All?"

[13]John G. Stackhouse Jr., *Humble Apologetics* (New York: Oxford University Press, 2002), p. 43. He goes on to cite Frederica Mathewes-Green, who notes several bloopers in major American publications, such *The Washington Post*, *Harper's* and *Newsweek*. The latter, for example, depicts "Jesse Jackson holding hands with Bill and Hillary Rodham Clinton and 'reciting the fifty-first Psalm, David's prayer for mercy after he had been seduced by Bathsheba'" (Stackhouse, *Humble Apologetics*, pp. 43-44, quoting Frederica Mathewes-Green, "Psalm 23 and All That," *Christianity Today*, February 7, 2000, p. 82).

[14]See Francis A. Schaeffer, *The Mark of a Christian* (Downers Grove, Ill.: InterVarsity Press, 1968), for a fuller exposition of this theme.

Chapter 7: What a Harebrained Idea!

[1]By *naturalist* I mean one who believes that nature (matter) is all there is, not one who loves timid, woodland creatures!

[2]I have formulated and elaborated on this definition in James W. Sire, *Naming the Elephant: Worldview as a Concept* (Downers Grove, Ill.: InterVarsity Press, 2004); and I have used it identifying the worldviews of theism, deism, naturalism, nihil-

ism, Eastern pantheistic monism, New Age thought and postmodernism in *The Universe Next Door,* 4th ed. (Downers Grove, Ill.: InterVarsity Press, 2004).

[3]Alfred North Whitehead, *Science and the Modern World* (New York: Mentor, 1951), p. 49.

[4]William J. Wainwright, "Skepticism, Romanticism and Faith," in *God and the Philosophers: The Reconciliation of Faith and Reason,* ed. Thomas V. Morris (New York: Oxford University Press, 1994), p. 85.

[5]For a fuller elaboration of these worldview and others, see Sire, *Universe Next Door,* which details the worldviews of theism, deism, naturalism, nihilism, existentialism, Eastern pantheistic monism, New Age thought and postmodernism.

[6]Christian Smith and Melinda Lundquist Denton, *Soul Searching: The Religious and Spiritual Lives of American Teenagers* (New York: Oxford University Press, 2005), p. 165.

[7]Thomas Nagel, *The Last Word* (New York: Oxford University Press, 1997), p. 130. Citing philosopher John Lucas, Christian philosopher Alvin Plantinga says that "philosophical naturalism" is now the orthodoxy of the Western intellectual world (Plantinga, "Darwin, Mind and Meaning," <http://www.ucsb.edu/fscf/library/plantinga/dennett.html>).

[8]"My Pilgrimage from Atheism to Theism," Gary R. Habermas's interview with Antony Flew, appears in the Winter 2005 issue of *Philosophia Christi,* a journal of Christian philosophy, <www.biola.edu/philosophiachristi>.

[9]Thomas Woodward, *Doubts About Darwin: A History of Intelligent Design* (Grand Rapids, Mich.: Baker, 2003), notes this: "The percentage of the hard core of evolutionary sentiment in the United States—those who believe in macroevolution *with no intelligent guidance at all*—has been measured by Gallup polls as relatively small. Over the past fifteen years Gallup has repeatedly listed the percentage of those who hold to a 'recent creation' view (vaguely described by Gallup) to be about 40 to 45 percent, while the 'God-guided evolution' view garnered another 40 to 45 percent. The third category, holding to a strictly naturalistic evolution, in which there was no participation by a preexisting intelligence, has consistently hovered at or slightly under 10 percent" (p. 197).

[10]Julian Huxley, *Evolution After Darwin* (1960), quoted by Woodward, *Doubts About Darwin,* p. 34.

[11]Julian Huxley, "The Emergence of Darwinism," in *Evolution of Life,* ed. Sol Tax (Chicago: University of Chicago Press, 1960), p. 1, as quoted in Woodward, *Doubts About Darwin,* p. 35.

[12]Richard Dawkins, *The Blind Watchmaker* (New York: W. W. Norton, 1998), p. 6.

[13]Michael Behe, in a fascinating account of his own change of mind from a primitive form of *theistic evolution* to *design science,* says "Materialism is the water [most scientists] swim in, the tenet whose falsity is literally unimaginable" ("Scientific

Orthodoxies," *First Things* [December 2005], p. 100). This view from a proponent of design science is confirmed by Harvard Zoologist Richard Lewontin (see the quotation in this book on pp. 115-16).

[14]Some *biblical creationists* are willing to concede that the earth is ancient, but maintain that human beings were created without nonhuman ancestors.

[15]The practical results are, however, often much the same. The university mind is not open to hearing anything about God's relation to the "natural" world.

[16]Richard Dawkins made this frequently quoted (and criticized) statement in a book review in the *New York Times,* April 9, 1989. His rejoinder criticism can be found in "Ignorance Is No Crime," *Free Inquiry Magazine* 21, no. 3, or at <www.secularhumanism.org>. He comments, "Of course it *sounds* arrogant, but undisguised clarity is easily mistaken for arrogance. Examine the statement carefully and it turns out to be moderate, almost self-evidently true." Dawkins then explains why, adding "tormented, bullied and brainwashed" into the mix of causes for not believing the evolutionary story. The notion, however, that his outrageous statement is "almost self-evidently true" illustrates the power of Dawkins's own commitment to the evolutionary theory; it does not show the statement to be "almost self-evidently true," nor does the remainder of his essay "Ignorance Is No Crime."

[17]In August 2004 "for the first time in history an article favoring intelligent design was published in a *refereed biological journal,*" writes Tom Woodward in *C. S. Lewis Society Letter,* October 2004: Steve Meyer's article, passing the muster of three scientist referees, appeared in the *Proceedings of the Biological Society of Washington.* A postpublication "fury broke out in September, as the Biological Society distanced itself from the article, saying not only should it not have been published, but also, that no such article will be published in the future." The career of the scientist-editor of the *Proceedings* has subsequently been placed in jeopardy. Woodward refers readers to www.apologetics.org for several reports on the controversy.

[18]As this book went to press, this was a hot topic in the academy and the daily papers. There is no question that on both a popular and a professional level, design science has entered the field of science. Cambridge University Press published *Debating Design,* coedited by William Dembski and Michael Ruse; Michigan State University Press has published *Darwinism, Design and Public Education,* edited by John Angus Campbell and Stephen C. Meyer. On a popular level, twenty-five Public Broadcasting Stations have aired *Unlocking the Mystery of Life. Time* magazine's cover story, "Evolution Wars" (August 15, 2005), pp. 26-35, surveyed the current controversy and noted the entry of design science into the evolution debate, briefly profiling Michael Behe. Cornell University's acting president Hunter Rawlings "devoted his entire state of the university address to an impassioned attack on intelligent design" (*Chicago Tribune,* November 25, 2005, Section 1, p. 9). Frustrated by

the academic community's refusal to take intelligent design seriously, students at Cornell and some twenty-five other universities have formed on organization to air the issues, if not resolve the controversy. It is called IDEA (Intelligent Design and Evolution Awareness), a clever acronym emphasizing the intelligence of talking about intelligence (Ibid., pp. 1, 9).

[19]Woodward traces the history of the controversy in *Doubts About Darwin.*

[20]Ibid., chap. 1. Design-science advocate William A. Dembski explains how those arguing for design science can most effectively reply to their critics in "Winning by Design," *Touchstone,* July/August 2004, pp. 54-59. His advice reflects the same set of rhetorical concerns and responses as the present book.

[21]I have found the most help in understanding Genesis 1-2 in Henri Blocher's *In the Beginning: The Opening Chapters of Genesis* (Downers Grove, Ill.: InterVarsity Press, 1984).

[22]C. S. Lewis, *The Letters of C. S. Lewis,* ed. W. H. Lewis (London: Geoffrey Bles, 1966), p. 287.

[23]John Stackhouse says, "We should avoid the popular apologetic zones located at the beginning and the end of the Bible—'creation versus evolution' at the one end and apocalyptic themes of judgment and rescue, heaven and hell, at the other—if our neighbor is willing to look with us at the heart of the Bible: the gospel testimony to Jesus" (John G. Stackhouse Jr., *Humble Apologetics: Defending the Faith Today* [New York: Oxford University Press, 2002], p. 190). The problem is that often we must have some sort of answer for those who object to the Christian faith on the basis of their belief in naturalistic evolution.

[24]Dr. Thomas Woodward is a professor at Trinity College of Florida who teaches the history of science, communication and theology and is the author of *Doubts About Darwin.* His is also the founder and director of the C. S. Lewis Society. As an active apologist on university campuses in the United States and Europe, he often focuses on intelligent design as a way to interest atheists and agnostics in considering the possibility of a divine origin and meaning of the universe. In a personal communication, he responded to an earlier draft of this chapter. While he is in general agreement with much of my assessment of the issue, he challenges my dismissal of intelligent design as a useful apologetic tool for most Christians. Here is part of his critique, published with his permission:

"When a metaphysical naturalist is interacting with us, I think we have the strongest encouragement from Rom 1:20 and from current events (the whole phenomenon of macroevolution being questioned as a credible scientific theory by so many key scientists even beyond the Behes, Johnsons and Dembskis), to raise and vigorously pursue the 'puzzle of design.' Every Christian college student should memorize this statement of Dawkins (from chapter one of *The Blind Watchmaker*): 'Biology is the study of complicated things that give the appearance of having been designed for a purpose.' So the reality of design, and the natural perception of design is not the issue. What *is* the issue is whether a credible naturalistic explanation of how design arose is in hand. Anyone who knows the score right now—how many scientists are beginning to jump from the sinking ship of mutation/selection as the engine of macroevolution—should view this topic as one of the most *fruitful* areas of discussion anyone can have. [Here Woodward refers to the first chapter of *Origination of Organismal Form*, ed. Gerd B. Müller and Stuart A. Newman (Cambridge, Mass.: MIT Press, 2003.]

"Let's imagine I am witnessing to my atheist sophomore roommate who's studying English, or math, or even chemistry at Ohio State, and he says, 'Well, I've heard about this Behe guy. My dad told me all about it and how he's been disproved.' Should the Christian who's watched *Unlocking the Mystery of Life* [a video explaining design science] and maybe done some basic reading and been taught the basics of this conflict change the subject or meekly say, 'There's more to this than you think, but let's change the subject,' or some such reply?

"Of course, each person differs in his/her background and knowledge, but I would think that because there is such a rich literature now [see pp. 174-77 for some of this], and such a thick and interesting conversation going that the Christian should jump in and pursue the discussion. He should vigorously engage the subject with his roommate, assuming the gospel has already been presented, and assuming that the person of Jesus has already been properly emphasized as the most important topic of study.

"The reason I think the Christian should *engage* rather than *avoid* such a discussion is that here, uniquely in the 21st century Western cultures, metaphysics is fruitfully exposed as a key player in the basic assumed scientific 'public knowledge.'

"In other words, the minimal plausibility of macroevolution or naturalist 'origin of life' scenarios is not viewed any longer as just a matter of meek reception of expert opinion, but a matter of public plausibility. There is right now a very public/ national plausibility crisis, and concomitant conversation that has been triggered on this very topic. This trend is not receding and I think you can follow the dotted lines into the future. If anything, the cell is viewed with each passing year as more like an automated factory—clogged and jam-packed, with level upon level of molecular complexity.

"In other words, the atheist kid back in the dorm room should be challenged to watch that very night the *Unlocking the Mystery of Life* or *The Privileged Planet* videos, and the two roommates should then have a discussion and talk about the 'range of options' for a thinking student in dealing with this whole area and the spiritual implications. Since God is already endorsing the idea (Rom 1:20) that he has preprogrammed nature to whisper 'I'm here' intuitively when people look at nature's complexity, why should we allow the evolutionists (and I'm including the theistic evolutionists) a free pass, a 'no hassle zone,' with their notion that chance and necessity can explain all of this functional complexity?"

Woodward likens a Christian's use of the issue of evolution to Jesus' reference to the falling of the tower of Siloam and the killing of innocent people. Recent events and popular issues seen in the light of Christian faith point up the relevance and truth of the Christian understanding of reality.

The videos of *Unlocking the Mystery of Life* and *The Privileged Planet* can be secured from <www.illustramedia.com>.

[25]William Edgar, *Reasons of the Heart: Recovering Christian Persuasion* (Grand Rapids, Mich.: Baker, 1996), p. 112.

Chapter 8: Who Am I to Judge?

[1]I have given a short version of this story in James W. Sire, *The Universe Next Door*, 4th ed. (Downers Grove, Ill.: InterVarsity Press, 2004); see esp. chap. 9.

[2]Christian Smith with Melinda Lundquist Denton, *Soul Searching: The Religious and Spiritual Lives of American Teenagers* (New York: Oxford University Press, 2005), p. 165. This entire book, a tour de force of relevant sociological analysis, bears reading by every Christian with a responsibility for raising and influencing young people.

[3]This trend toward relativism is not new. In the 1960s it was already noted by Martin E. Marty and Daniel Boorstin. Marty writes, "The American culture is openly syncretistic. Many truths are presented by a pluralistic people and most of them, it is conceived, can be appropriated into one consensus. A mixed culture becomes, then, a blurred culture. 'We expect to go to a "church of our choice" and yet feel its guiding power over us; to revere God and to be God. . . . We expect everybody to believe deeply in his religion, yet not to think less of others for not believing.'" (Martin E. Marty, *Varieties of Unbelief* [Garden City, N.Y.: Image Books, 1966] quoting Daniel Boorstin, *The Image* [New York: Atheneum, 1962], p. 4.)

[4]Ibid., p. 145.

[5]Ibid., p. 144.

[6]Ibid.

[7]Harold Netland, once a student of John Hick, has brilliantly analyzed Hick's attempt to justify his notion of "pluralism" (Hick's term for what I take to be a sophisticated attempt to avoid the obvious objections to relativism). See Netland's *Dissonant Voices* (Grand Rapids, Mich.: Eerdmans, 1991) and *Encountering Religious Pluralism: The Challenge to Christian Faith and Mission* (Downers Grove, Ill.: InterVarsity Press, 2001).

[8]Aristotle *Metaphysics* 1.1.

[9]I have written about this in chaps. 5 and 6 in *Chris Chrisman Goes to College* (Downers Grove, Ill.: InterVarsity Press, 1993), pp. 45-68.

[10]"Ten Myths: Campus Is Engaged," a report circulated by Mark and Gwen Potter, staff members for InterVarsity Christian Fellowship (Fall 1991).

[11]See chapter eleven below for a fuller explanation of this end run, or my *Why Should Anyone Believe Anything at All?* (Downers Grove, Ill.: InterVarsity Press, 1994) for a book-length version.

[12]See, for example, Netland, *Dissonant Voices*, and the essays in the following two collections: Alan R. Malachowski, ed., *Reading Rorty: Critical Responses to "Philosophy and the Mirror of Nature" (and Beyond)* (Oxford: Blackwell, 1990), and Robert R. Brandom, ed., *Rorty and His Critics* (Oxford: Blackwell, 2000).

[13]J. Budziszewski, "Practical Responses to Relativism and Postmodernism, Part 1," in *Philosophy: Christian Perspectives for the New Millennium,* ed. Paul Copan, Scott B. Luley and Stan Wallace (Addison, Tex.: CIM / Norcross, Ga.: RZIM, 2003), p. 94.

[14]Ibid.

[15]Richard Rorty, *Philosophy and Social Hope* (London: Penguin, 1999).

[16]In a similar vein, philosopher Roy Clouser comments on the pretheoretical commitment of some forms of both Hinduism and Buddhism: "Because perception and logic lead to and/or support belief in the existence of many things, all percepts are rejected as illusions and all concepts are rejected as false. (Thus the very beliefs that thinkers such as Aristotle and Descartes took to be infallibly true are said to be infallibly false!)" (Roy Clouser, *Knowing with the Heart: Religious Experience and Belief in God* [Downers Grove, Ill.: InterVarsity Press, 1999], p. 78).

[17]Ibid., p. 62.

[18]Richard Lewontin, "Billions and Billions of Demons," review of *The Demon-Haunted World: Science as a Candle in the Dark* by Carl Sagan, *New York Review of Books,* January 9, 1997, quoted from <www.csus.edu/indiv/m/mayesgr/Lewontin1.htm>. See Victor Reppert's comments in *C.S. Lewis's Dangerous Idea: In Defense of the Argument from Reason* (Downers Grove, Ill.: 2003), p. 125.

Chapter 9: The Heart Wants What It Wants

[1]Augustine *Confessions* 10.23.

[2]Nancy Pearcey, *Total Truth* (Wheaton, Ill.: Crossway, 2004), p. 321.

[3]John G. Stackhouse Jr., *Humble Apologetics: Defending the Faith Today* (New York: Oxford University Press, 2002), p. 146.

[4]For example, Jesus' bold claim in Matthew 11:27 comes after he has referred to his healing in 11:1-6.

[5]Pearcey, *Total Truth,* p. 126.

[6]A serious response to the first of these has already been suggested in chapters one and three (pp. 27, 52-54). The second is harder to reply to since it poses a conundrum. If the story is taken as legend or myth, of course, there is no problem. But if the story is taken as literal history, how could Cain have a wife if he and Abel were Adam and Eve's only children? Of course, the Bible does say that they had other children (Gen 5:4); his wife could have been a sister. The incest taboo began as prohibiting sexual relations between parents and children and only later extended to relations between brother and sister. But rather than take this rather anthropological approach, I suggest it is better simply to acknowledge that the Bible makes no attempt to deal with this question and so neither will you. We must deal with what ancient texts say, not what they omit. Surely if there were anything important to be learned from how Cain got his wife, we would have been told. The point of the opening chapters of Genesis is to deal with the purposeful origin of human life as created by God. The richness of the implications of what we are told about human origins are scarcely exhausted by all our attempts to understand them. For more detail on the specific issue of Cain's wife, see Walter C. Kaiser Jr., Peter H. David, F. F. Bruce and Manfred T. Branch, *Hard Sayings of the Bible* (Downers Grove, Ill.: InterVarsity Press, 1996), p. 101. For one especially wise commentary, see "Human Origins" in Derek Kidner's *Genesis: An Introduction and Commentary,* Tyndale Old Testament Commentaries (Downers Grove, Ill.: InterVarsity Press, 1967), pp. 26-31.

The third comment is primarily a challenge to your authority and is in fact misdirected. Your reply can be something like this: "It is not my judgment that you need to be worried about. It is rather what the Bible, or Jesus in the Bible, says. Look with me and see what the Bible or Jesus says." Then you can point them to passages like John 3:16-21; 5:28-30; Matthew 25:31-46; Luke 13:1-5. The stress, however, should be on God's gracious forgiveness; no one is necessarily bound to end in hell. See the comments on hell in chapter four (pp. 57-60) above.

[7]J. Budziszewski, "Practical Responses to Relativism and Postmodernism, Part 2," in *Philosophy: Christian Perspectives for the New Millennium,* ed. Paul Copan, Scott B. Luley and Stan Wallace (Addison, Tex.: CIM / Norcross, Ga.: RZIM, 2003) pp. 104-5.

[8]Ibid., pp. 105-6.

Chapter 10: I See You Are Very Religious

[1]Eckhard J. Schnabel, *Paul and the Early Church,* vol. 2 of *Early Christian Mission* (Downers Grove, Ill.: InterVarsity Press, 2004), p. 1178.

[2]For a more sophisticated and richer analysis of Paul's address to the Athenian philosophers, see Schnabel's masterful analysis, ibid., pp. 1392-1404.

[3]E. M. Blaiklock, *The Acts of the Apostles,* Tyndale New Testament Commentaries (Grand Rapids, Mich.: Eerdmans, 1959), p. 138.

[4]Schnabel, *Paul and the Early Church,* pp. 1399-1400.

[5]Blaiklock, *Acts of the Apostles,* p. 141.

[6]Schnabel, *Paul and the Early Church,* p. 1401.

[7]Socrates was tried by the Areopagus hundreds of years earlier (Craig Keener, *The IVP Bible Background Commentary* [Downers Grove, Ill.: InterVarsity Press, 1993], p. 373).

[8]*International Herald Tribune,* November 18, 1991, p. 1.

[9]Christian Smith and Melinda Lundquist Denton, *Soul Searching: The Religious and Spiritual Lives of American Teenagers* (New York: Oxford University Press, 2005).

[10]Jason Boffetti, "How Richard Rorty Found Religion," *First Things,* May 2004, p. 29.

[11]Daniel Dennett, *Darwin's Dangerous Idea: Evolution and the Meanings of Life* (New York: Simon & Schuster, 1995), pp. 535-36.

[12]Richard Dawkins tries to excuse the "arrogance and intolerance" of this statement in "Ignorance Is No Crime," *Free Inquiry,* 21, no. 3, where he says, "Of course, it *sounds* arrogant, but undisguised clarity is easily mistaken for arrogance. Examine the statement carefully and it turns out to be moderate, almost self-evidently true" (available at <www.secularhumanism.org/library/fi/dawkins21_3.html>).

Chapter 11: So Why Should I Believe Anything?

[1]The idea of a survey came in 1989 from Mark and Gwen Potter, InterVarsity staff members serving Bryn Mawr and Haverford colleges.

Chapter 12: Framing Effective Arguments

[1]Lewis recognized the apologetic value of scholarship done by Christians: "The first step to the re-conversion of this country [England] is a series, produced by Christians, which can beat the *Penguin* and the *Thinkers Library* on their own ground" (C. S. Lewis, "Christain Apologetics," in *God in the Dock: Essays on Theology and Ethics,* ed. Walter Hooper [Grand Rapids, Mich.: Eerdmans, 1970], p. 101).

[2]Lyle W. Dorsett calls Lewis a "literary evangelist" (*The Essential C. S. Lewis* [New York: Collins, 1988], p. 8; and Lewis himself once remarked that "any amount of theology can be smuggled into people's minds under the cover of romance without their knowing it" (*The Letters of C. S. Lewis,* ed. W. H. Lewis [London: Geoffrey Bles, 1966], p. 167.

[3]This pattern of "presuppositional apologetics" derives from Cornelius Van Til. Francis Schaeffer learned it from Van Til and then modified it. I picked it up from Schaeffer. The clearest explanation of Van Til's method and its theoretical underpinnings is found in Greg L. Bahnsen's *Van Til's Apologetic: Readings and Analysis* (Phillipsburg, N.J.: P&R Publishing, 1998), esp. 489-520.

Author Index

Subject Index

Scripture Index